MW01025572

Adventuring in Paradise

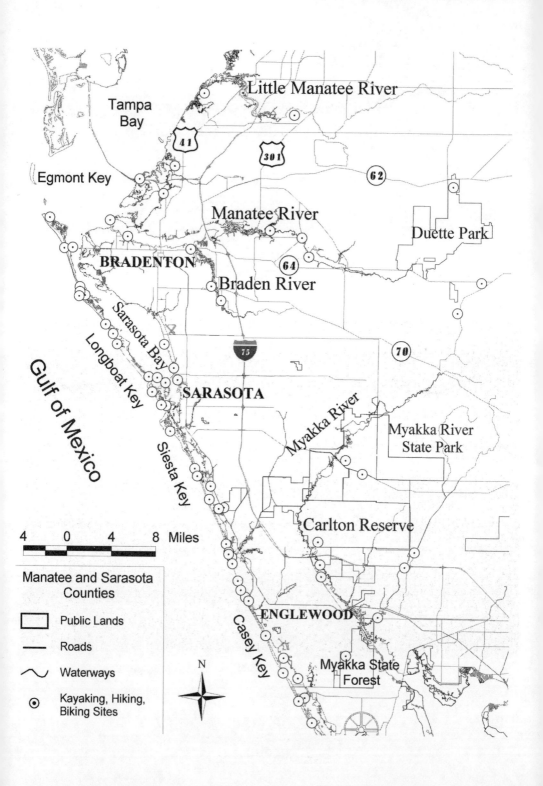

Adventuring in Paradise

Hiking/Paddling/Biking/Walking
in Sarasota and Manatee Counties, Florida

Gene Jones

Photographs by JH Pete Carmichael
Maps by Joe Jacobson, Sarasota County Environmental Services

Pineapple Press, Inc.
Sarasota, Florida

Caution

Y̶ou must take responsibility for yourself and your companions when enjoy-
ing the outdoors, as outdoor recreation can be hazardous. Some hazards are
mentioned in this book, but the listed hazards are not all-inclusive. You must
take responsibility to identify and manage hazards associated with your activity. You must recognize the limitations of your ability and equipment and act
accordingly. For example, a Gulf of Mexico paddle in moderate conditions may be
safe for an experienced sea kayaker while foolhardy and unsafe for a canoeist.
Always put safety first. You must be physically fit and have the skill, technique, and
proper equipment to safely perform your activity. Do not expect to read this book
and know all you need to know to be safe. This book is not intended as a primer
to teach you skills or techniques. Take lessons from a certified instructor.

The information in this book was accurate at publication, but conditions
change constantly. Laws, ordinances, and rules change and currently available
facilities become unavailable to the public. Even natural environments can
change radically—New Pass did not exist until a hurricane opened the pass in
1848. Consequently, as you plan your outdoor activity, verify the information is
still correct before you set out. The listed resources should save time doing so.

Copyright © 2003 by Gene Jones

All rights reserved. No part of this book may be reproduced in any form or by
any means, electronic or mechanical, including photocopying, recording, or by
any information storage and retrieval system, without permission in writing
from Pineapple Press.

Inquiries should be addressed to:
Pineapple Press, Inc.
P.O. Box 3889
Sarasota, FL 34230

www.pineapplepress.com

Library of Congress Cataloging-in-Publication Data

Jones, Gene, 1945–.
    Adventuring in Paradise : hiking/paddling/biking/walking in Sarasota
and Manatee counties, Florida / Gene Jones.— 1st ed.
        p. cm.
    Includes bibliographical references (p.).
    ISBN 1-56164-280-0 (pbk. : alk. paper)
        1. Outdoor recreation—Florida—Sarasota County—Guidebooks. 2.
Outdoor recreation—Florida—Manatee County—Guidebooks. 3. Sarasota
County (Fla.)—Guidebooks. 4. Manatee County (Fla.)—Guidebooks. I. Title.

GV191.42.F6 J66 2003
796'.0975961—dc21

                                                                        2003001048
First Edition
10 9 8 7 6 5 4 3 2 1

Design by Shé Sicks
Printed in the United States of America

All royalties from the sale of this book benefit the
Manatee-Sarasota Group of the Florida Chapter of the Sierra Club

Acknowledgments

Many friends offered encouragement and advice, but several had the unusual patience to provide information and suggestions. Special thanks to Terry Proeger, George Keiser, Laura Pether, George and Nancy Wettlaufer, Steve Ross, and June and David Cussen and the others at Pineapple Press. Particular thanks to Joe Jacobson for the maps and Peter Carmichael for the photographs. Thanks also to those county and state employees who provided information and advice. Compiling this booklet confirmed how fortunate we are in Sarasota and Manatee Counties to have many park and recreation department employees conscientiously striving to protect the environment while simultaneously providing public use to wonderful habitats. Likewise, the same can be said for many state park and forestry employees.

Kudos to Bob Richardson for initiating the project and to the Manatee-Sarasota Group for sticking with it.

Last, but not least, thanks to my family for their support and help. My wife, Judy, had the patience to visit every potential kayak launch in the two counties. My daughter, Erika, had excellent editing ideas and tried to keep me from "preaching" about environmental protection. Finally, thanks to all of you who enjoy and protect the outdoors. See you there.

Contents

Northern

Sites

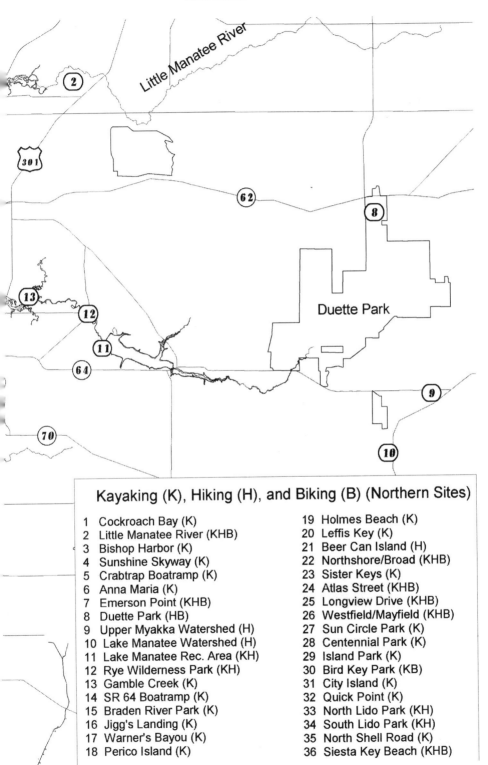

Kayaking (K), Hiking (H), and Biking (B) (Northern Sites)

1 Cockroach Bay (K)
2 Little Manatee River (KHB)
3 Bishop Harbor (K)
4 Sunshine Skyway (K)
5 Crabtrap Boatramp (K)
6 Anna Maria (K)
7 Emerson Point (KHB)
8 Duette Park (HB)
9 Upper Myakka Watershed (H)
10 Lake Manatee Watershed (H)
11 Lake Manatee Rec. Area (KH)
12 Rye Wilderness Park (KH)
13 Gamble Creek (K)
14 SR 64 Boatramp (K)
15 Braden River Park (K)
16 Jigg's Landing (K)
17 Warner's Bayou (K)
18 Perico Island (K)

19 Holmes Beach (K)
20 Leffis Key (K)
21 Beer Can Island (H)
22 Northshore/Broad (KHB)
23 Sister Keys (K)
24 Atlas Street (KHB)
25 Longview Drive (KHB)
26 Westfield/Mayfield (KHB)
27 Sun Circle Park (K)
28 Centennial Park (K)
29 Island Park (K)
30 Bird Key Park (KB)
31 City Island (K)
32 Quick Point (K)
33 North Lido Park (KH)
34 South Lido Park (KH)
35 North Shell Road (K)
36 Siesta Key Beach (KHB)

Southern Sites

Note: Site descriptions, pages 21–87, are keyed to Northern and Southern maps, for example:

Kayaking(K), Hiking(H), and Biking(B)
Southern Sites

37 Turtle Beach/Palmer Point (KHB)
38 Midnight Pass (K)
39 Osprey Fishing Pier (K)
40 Blackburn Point Park (KB)
41 Shoreland Park (K)
42 Oscar Scherer (KHB)
43 Myakka River State Park (KHB)
44 Myakka Prairie (HB)
45 Carlton Reserve (KHB)
46 Myakkahatchee Park (KHB)
47 Oaks Park (KHB)
48 Snook Haven (K)
49 Jelks Tract (H)
50 Nokomis Beach (K)
51 North & South Jetties (KH)
52 Higel Marine Park (K)
53 Venice Beach (KH)
54 Service Park (KH)
55 Brohard Park (K)
56 Casperson Beach (KHB)
57 Shamrock Park (HB)
58 Manasota Beach (KH)
59 Lemon Bay Park (KH)
60 Blind Pass (KHB)
61 Indian Mound Park (K)
62 Englewood Beach (KH)
63 Lemon Bay Boat Ramp (K)
64 Stump Pass (KHB)
65 Myakka State Forest (KHB)
66 Marina Park (K)

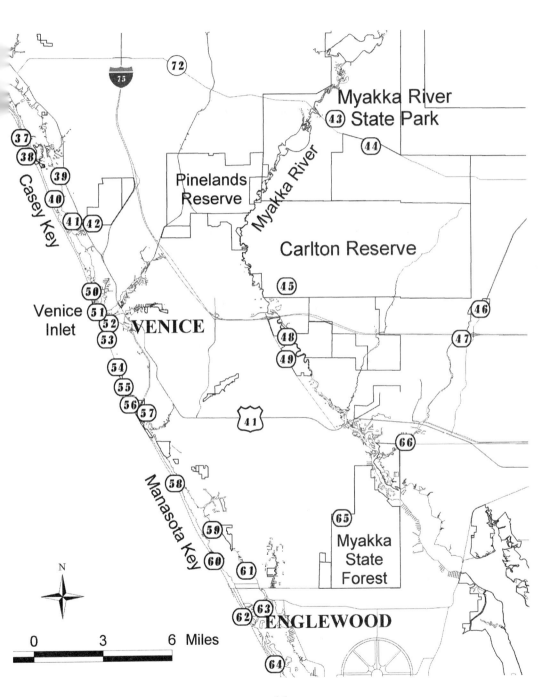

Myakka River State Park

Pinelands Reserve

Myakka River

Carlton Reserve

Casey Key

Venice Inlet

VENICE

Manasota Key

Myakka State Forest

ENGLEWOOD

N

0   3   6 Miles

37
38
39
40
41 42
50
51
52
53
54
55
56
57
58
59
60
61
62 63
64
72
43
44
45
46
47
48
49
41
65
66

Overview

Located south of Tampa Bay on the Gulf of Mexico, Sarasota and Manatee Counties are best known for their unique combination of white sand beaches and culture. The beaches are world class, while institutions like Mote Marine Laboratory, Marie Selby Botanical Gardens, the Asolo Center for the Performing Arts, Sarasota Opera Company, Sarasota Ballet, Ringling Museum, Ringling School of Art and Design, and New College at the University of South Florida give the area a well-deserved reputation as a cultural center for Florida.

Perhaps due to the area's heavy urbanization, many assume that Sarasota and Manatee Counties offer little outdoor recreation except beautiful beaches. After all, both counties are largely developed. No national parks or forests exist in the two counties. The two counties have a combined population of 589,959 (2000 census) and more than 10,000 people move to the area each year. Tourists and part-time residents increase the population by up to a third. Little wonder that Sarasota/Manatee is not considered a Mecca for outdoor recreation. Most outdoor guides hardly mention the area.

Yet to dismiss Sarasota/Manatee as unsuitable for outdoor adventure is a mistake. Opportunity for high-quality outdoor adventure exists, but you must look beyond the condominiums and development to find it. For example, Myakka State Park is one of the largest state parks in Florida and the Myakka River is designated as a Wild and Scenic River. Relatively pristine coastline along the Gulf of Mexico and bays still exists. Several areas have been named Outstanding Florida Waters. Located in the

13

transition zone between temperate and tropical climates, most of the habitats that exist in Florida can be found in Sarasota or Manatee County. In fact, ecologists recognize over twenty different native habitats in Sarasota and Manatee Counties, some of which are unique to Florida.

Birds you may expect to see in the various habitats are mentioned because bird populations often indicate environmental health. The absence of typical birds can mean an area is degraded, fragmented, or polluted. Many birds found in this area are simply beautiful to see. Your life will be richer if you are familiar with them.

HABITATS

FLATWOODS

Very common locally, flatwoods are characterized by slash pines and saw palmetto. Shrubs such as wax myrtle, groundsel, and gallberry are common. Grasses and wildflowers proliferate. The flatwoods require fire to stay healthy, and public lands are managed using fire as a maintenance tool. Common mammals found in the flatwoods are bobcats, fox, opossum, armadillos, and feral pigs. Whitetail deer and fox squirrel may be found in the larger flatwoods tracts. Some common birds found in the flatwoods are the eastern towhee, catbird, and mockingbird.

HIGH PINE

Almost all high pine forest in Sarasota and Manatee County has been logged or replaced by development. Pines and low shrubs characterize the high pines ecosystem. Like the flatwoods, the high pine ecosystem requires fire to keep healthy. Wiregrass, exotic bahia grass, ferns, and wildflowers may carpet the forest floor in open areas. The same animals seen in the flatwoods also thrive in high pines. Common birds are blue jay, cardinal, and palm warbler.

DRY PRAIRIE

Open, flat land with few trees characterizes prairie in Florida. Low-growing saw palmetto is the predominant shrub. Many plants found in the flatwoods also grow on the prairies. Although at a higher elevation than marsh, the soil is often wet with standing water in the rainy season. The prairie needs occasional fire to maintain a treeless expanse. Sandhill cranes, quail, hawks, and burrowing owls like the prairie habitat. Myakka State Park has large areas that are being managed to restore dry prairie after years of fire suppression.

SCRUB

The scrub habitat unique to Florida is a threatened ecosystem. With high, well-drained sandy soil, the scrub ecosystem has been mostly destroyed by housing and agricultural development. Sand pines predominate while the understory consists of evergreen shrubs, like scrub oak. Because the scrub soils are well drained, the scrub microclimate can be desertlike in the hot subtropical sun. Scrub plants and animals often have similar adaptations to those found in western deserts. Many threatened and endangered species, both plant and animal, can be found in the scrub, for example the gopher tortoise, scrub jay, scrub lizard, indigo snake, and coontie. Scrub can be found at Oscar Scherer State Park and Little Manatee State Recreation Area.

MESIC HAMMOCK

Broadleaf trees like oak and sabal palm characterize the mesic hammock locally. These hammocks can tolerate occasional flooding. Expect to see epiphytes, Spanish moss, and ferns in the trees in this moist habitat.

WET PRAIRIE AND FRESHWATER MARSH

Often found along rivers, wet prairies and freshwater marshes are flat areas without trees and are subject to periodic flooding. Grasses like maiden cane predominate. The area along the Myakka River between the Upper and Lower Myakka Lakes typifies this habitat.

CYPRESS DOME

Often associated with pine flatwoods and marshes, cypress domes are quite picturesque. Larger cypress trees grow in the center with tree size gradually diminishing outward to the dome's edges as if the trees were trimmed. Cypress, including its mulched bark, is very valuable. As a result, most cypress has been logged except in protected areas. The loss of cypress habitat probably contributed to the extinction of the ivory-billed woodpecker. Wood ducks like to nest in cypress domes. A cypress dome can be found at Myakka State Park.

Mangrove Swamp

Mangroves are saltwater-tolerant trees that flourish in Sarasota and Manatee Counties. Mangroves are cold sensitive and easily killed by frost. There are four types of mangrove. The red mangrove, called the "walking tree" by Native Americans, is readily identified by its prop roots. Black mangroves have numerous pneumatophores, fingerlike projections from the ground. White mangroves and buttonwood are sometimes found behind the red and the black as ground level rises. The mangrove forest forms the base of the estuarine food chain and serves as nursery grounds for fish, crabs, and shrimp. Common birds found in the mangrove swamps are ospreys, cormorants, and wading birds. Raccoons may be seen climbing around the prop roots looking for oysters and other seafood. Manatees seek refuge in the tidal lagoons within mangrove swamps.

Salt Marsh

Salt marshes are shallow areas in the estuaries where creeks and rivers flow into the Gulf. They are generally treeless and grassy. Tidal creeks meander through them, flooding the marshes at high tide. Fiddler crabs scurry around the flats at low tide in unpolluted areas. Many local salt marshes have been filled for housing.

Coastal Beach

White sand barrier island beaches are a prime tourist attraction in Sarasota and Manatee Counties. These beaches are dynamic, and most are eroding or accreting. Millions of dollars are spent to renourish the sand on some beaches. At barrier island beaches, exotic trees like Australian Pine tend to predominate. Sea oats often grow on low dunes. Numerous shore birds and pelicans are common. Bottlenose dolphins often cavort and feed near shore, while sea turtles use the beaches for nesting in the summer.

Sea Grass Beds

Sea grass beds are extensive because the area has many large shallow bays. Sea grass habitats are very biologically productive and are necessary nurseries for fish and other marine life. For years, pollution from sewage treatment plants and other sources killed the grass beds. Since pollution has been reduced, the grass beds have made a dramatic resurgence in recent years, especially in Sarasota Bay.

Hiking

Generally, hiking in Sarasota and Manatee Counties rates as easy to moderate. Hiking is generally over level ground, often no more physically difficult than walking on the beach. Rarely will you be more than a few miles from a road or place to seek assistance if needed. Nevertheless, the hiker should follow general rules of hiking and be alert to a few local hazards.

Protect your feet. Light hiking boots are recommended. The most common hiking injury is foot injury that can be avoided by wearing boots. Hiking boots provide ankle support and also protect from several local plants that can abrade your feet. Sandals, open-toed shoes, and low-cut shoes like running shoes may not be adequate. Some cuts are an annoyance, others can be more serious. A sandspur prick is just a nuisance while a stab from a Spanish bayonet can be very painful and subject to infection. Either makes your hike unnecessarily unpleasant.

Hiking boots also provide some protection from snakebite. The majority of snakebites are on the foot, which sometimes can be thwarted by a sturdy boot. If you hike the backcountry in Sarasota and Manatee County, chances are you will step near a snake. Hikers have stepped right over snakes, even poisonous ones, without seeing the snake until companions pointed it out. Luckily, snakes rarely bite hikers, but you could meet the ornery one. Watch your step.

Waterproof boots are desirable because you will likely walk through wet areas or water.

Long pants are also recommended. Shorts are certainly more comfortable on a hot day, but you run a risk of scratching your legs. Some plants can cut or scratch and can grow across a trail only days after a trail has been cleared. One of the most common shrubs is the saw palmetto with serrated stems that easily cut bare skin.

You will be hiking in a subtropical environment. Even in mid-winter, the heat index (heat and humidity) can reach the danger level. Protect yourself from sunburn and overheating. Wear a hat. Take water and food. Go easy until you acclimatize. Hikers can "bonk" from not drinking enough to maintain hydration and not eating enough to maintain energy.

Insects can be a nuisance. Mosquitoes can be vicious in some places, especially in summer. Have insect repellent available. Exotic fire ants have a very painful bite and swarm their victim. Fire ant bites can cause a severe reaction in those allergic to the ant's venom. Scorpions and poisonous spiders also live in the area. Watch where you stand and sit.

Some hikes are remote, so hikers can become disoriented because the terrain is flat and landmarks are not always visible. A little disorientation can turn a short hike into an unpleasantly long one. Take map and compass and know how to use them. Take a rudimentary first aid kit.

Local mammals are not threatening if you keep your distance. Mammals you are apt to see, like deer, hogs, coyotes, or bobcats, have rarely, if ever, attacked hikers. The elusive and rare Florida panther could be present as well as the black bear. You'll be exceptionally lucky to see either.

On the other hand, a common local reptile can be dangerous. The Florida alligator is abundant and large ones can be dangerous. In areas where alligators have become accustomed to people, they can become aggressive, particularly if they have been fed. In 1973, a teenage girl was attacked and killed in the swimming area at Oscar Scherer State Park by a thirteen-foot alligator, which had been fed. DO NOT FEED ANY WILDLIFE.

Follow good hiking practices. Take only pictures; leave only tracks.

MYAKKA RIVER STATE PARK $\boxed{S-43}$

Location: 13207 S.R. 72, Sarasota, FL, 34241, 17 miles east of Sarasota (exit 205, I-75) on State Road 72.

Phone: (941) 361-6511, Email: Myakka@netsrq.com

Website: www.myakka.sarasota.fl.us

Facilities: Rest rooms and water are located at the entrance station, at the concession at Upper Myakka Lake, and at the Clay Gully picnic area. The park has two RV/tent campgrounds, rental cabins, and six primitive campgrounds. Entrance fee.

Hours: 8:00 A.M. to sunset.

Highlights: Nearly forty miles of hiking trails crisscross the park traversing several different habitats such as dry prairie, hammock, marshes, and swamp. Wildlife and wildflowers are abundant. The Myakka ecosystem can be viewed from a seventy-foot tower and canopy walk.

Myakka Park is one of the largest Florida state parks with 28,876 acres. A small visitor center highlights plants and animals found in the park. The park has two large lakes, the Upper Myakka Lake and Lower Myakka Lake. Numerous ponds and sloughs are scattered throughout the park. The Myakka River, designated as a Florida Wild and Scenic River, bisects the park from north to south, connecting the Upper and Lower Lakes. The Florida Trails Association maintains nearly forty miles of hiking trails within the park. An old railroad grade and power line cross the park providing direct routes to the park interior. Trail maps are available at the ranger station entrance.

The hiking trails are located to the east of Upper Myakka Lake and the paved park roads, Park Drive and North Drive. Hiking trails pass through a wide variety of habitats, but the most common are flatwoods, hammocks, and prairie.

Six primitive campsites without facilities and only non-potable water are scattered throughout the park (Prairie Campsite has no water). Permits must be obtained to camp at these sites.

A short handicapped-accessible nature trail begins at Park Drive just north of the Myakka River Bridge and winds through a typical hammock and slough. Near the nature trail, a canopy walk with a seventy-foot tower provides an overview of the park ecosystem and access to the tree canopy.

The lake and riverine environments found at Myakka State Park are a tremendous attraction for birds. At times, bird watching at Myakka State Park may be better than famous birding "hot spots" like the Everglades. You cannot visit Myakka without seeing resident waterbirds like anhingas, egrets, snowy egrets, great blue herons, tricolored herons, little blue herons, green herons, ibis, kingfishers, and ospreys. Other waterbirds commonly seen along the coast, like sandpipers, black-necked stilts, and black skimmers, can sometimes be seen at the park. Pink roseate spoonbills often add color to the lakeshore.

The habitat variety in the park attracts many migrating birds as well. Large birds like hawks, eagles, white pelicans, turkeys, and sandhill cranes either reside in or migrate through the park. Only an expert could identify all the smaller birds you may see, as over 250 bird species have been identified in the park. A bird walk located at the edge of Upper Myakka Lake along North Drive provides excellent bird watching. Volunteers are sometimes at the boardwalk to assist with bird identification.

Myakka Park teems with alligators. You're unlucky if you don't see several. Good observation points for alligators are the Park Drive Bridge and the dam at the south end of Upper Myakka Lake. Alligators may be encountered on the hiking trails, especially around the sloughs and ponds.

For the more venturesome, a permit can be obtained at the entrance station to hike in the Wilderness Preserve to the Lower Myakka Lake and Deep Hole. There are no trails in the Wilderness Preserve—dirt roads provide foot access. At its shortest, a hike to the Lower Lake is about five miles roundtrip. During low water you can often hike along the lake bank. A shady hammock borders the lake and is passable except during high water. Wildlife is usually more abundant in the preserve than in other areas of the park. Expect to get your feet wet on this hike except during the driest times.

Larger mammals living in the park are hogs, deer, foxes, raccoons, bobcats, and coyotes. Black bears and panthers have been sighted occasionally.

Get Involved:
Friends of the Myakka River, Inc.
1312 S. Orange Ave.
Sarasota, FL 34239
www.myakka.sarasota.fl.us./friends.html

The Florida Trail Association
P.O. Box 13708
Gainesville, FL 32604
www.fta.org

To be a park volunteer, contact the park superintendent.

MYAKKA PRAIRIE

Location: Adjacent to Myakka State Park's eastern boundary. Access from State Road 72.

Facilities: none.

Hours: 8:00 A.M. to Sunset.

Highlights: Myakka Prairie is a 8,249-acre tract containing prairie, depression ponds, and hammock habitats. Permits to enter must be obtained at the Myakka State Park entrance station.

Though owned by Southwest Florida Water Management District, the property is managed by Myakka State Park. Used for pasture and agriculture prior to its purchase by the Water Management District, much of the property has not reverted to natural habitat. Dirt roads provide access to the interior, but there are no trails. In the areas not cleared for pasture, the ecology is similar to non-riverine habitats in Myakka State Park.

DUETTE PARK N–8

Location: 2649 Rawls Rd., RR2, Bowling Green, FL. From Parrish in Manatee County Take State Road 62 east for about 20 miles to Duette Road. Go about 3 miles to Duette Road. Turn south on Duette Road and continue to entrance gate (look for signage on SR 62 and Duette Road).

Phone: (941) 776-2295

Facilities: Toilets, no water. Tent camping is available on weekends, no electricity or water. Entrance fees are charged and you must be issued a permit.

Hours: Call to verify when the park is open. Currently it closes Mondays and Tuesdays. It is open Wednesday through Thursday 8:00 A.M. to noon. On Friday, Saturday, and Sunday it is open 8:00 A.M. to 4:00 P.M. Once in the park you can stay until sunset. Hiking is limited to the months of December and March through August. The park is open to hunting during season.

Highlights: Duette Park is a 24,000-acre Manatee County watershed and conservation land management park. This park is the headwaters for the Manatee River. It contains diverse ecosystems including dry prairie, oak hammock, marsh, pine forest, and scrub. Deer, hog, bobcat, and gray fox are abundant. You may see eagles, turkeys, or scrub jays. Threatened species like gopher tortoises and indigo snakes inhabit the park. Big alligators over ten feet live in the park although they're not ubiquitous like in Myakka State Park.

While no trails are specifically designated as hiking trails, you can hike shell and dirt roads that crisscross the park. The most interesting but more difficult hiking is along the riverine ecosystems where creeks flow through the park. You may have to bushwhack and find your own trail. Don't get lost. Make sure you have a map and compass.

This park is as remote as you can find in Manatee and Sarasota Counties. Fill your gas tank before going and take food and water when you visit.

RYE WILDERNESS PARK (N–12)

Location: 905 Rye Rd., Parrish, FL. From I-75 travel east on State Road 64 approximately four miles; turn north on Rye Road; continue on Rye Road approximately six miles to the park.

Phone: (941) 776-0900

Facilities: Restrooms, tent camping with showers for campers.

Hours: Office hours are 3:00 P.M. to 7:00 P.M. Friday and Saturday. Most sections of the park are accessible from dawn to sunset every day.

Highlights: Though only 145 acres, the park is worth exploring because of the beautiful hardwood forest along the Upper Manatee River, which bisects the park. Several short trails go to the river. Bobcat, gray fox, and deer may be seen. Also look for eagles and gopher tortoises.

OSCAR SCHERER STATE PARK (S-42)

Location: 1843 S. Tamiami Trail (U.S. 41), Osprey, FL, 34229. Approximately ten miles south of downtown Sarasota.

Phone: (941) 483-5956

Facilities: Water and restrooms are available at the ranger station at the entrance to the park and at Lake Osprey. Full facility RV camping and a group campground are available. No primitive camping is available. Entrance fee.

Hours: 8:00 A.M. till sunset.

Highlights: Totally surrounded by suburban development, Oscar Scherer State Park has nearly 1400 acres containing several natural habitats. An important habitat in the park is the scubby flatwoods habitat. Found only in Florida, this habitat is rapidly disappearing in Florida except in protected lands. A population of scrub jays, a threatened bird species, lives in the park. South Creek bisects the park. The park has several small lakes and one, Lake Osprey, has a designated swimming area.

Oscar Scherer State Park provides an excellent overview of several habitats in a small area. Within a few hours, you can hike through scrubby flatwoods, pine flatwoods, shady hammocks, marsh, and along a tidal creek and spring-fed lake. There are over fifteen miles of hiking trails that wind through the park.

Hiking the trails, you will probably encounter scrub jays.

Scrub jays have unique behavioral traits. Quite tame, they will sometimes gather around you if you stand quietly. Scrub jays live in cooperative groups and stay in one area for generations. As Sarasota County Commissioner Jon Thaxton noted in the brochure *Florida Scrub Jays at Oscar Scherer State Park,* " . . . it is conceivable that some Florida scrub jay properties have remained in the same family longer than any human-owned land in the state." Resist the temptation to feed these attractive birds.

The variety of birds and animals found at Oscar Scherer State Park is outstanding. Over 160 bird species have been identified in the park. Other animals identified in the park are sixteen amphibian species, five turtle species, eight lizard species, eighteen snake species, twenty-seven mammal species, and alligators. In addition to the threatened scrub jay, other species found in the park with a declining population are the gopher tortoise, gopher frog, and indigo snake.

The Lester Finley Nature Trail, a short (half-mile), handicapped-accessible shell nature trail, meanders along South Creek at the transition zone from fresh to salt water. Very well done, this trail is one of the better nature trails in the area.

Get Involved: The Friends of Oscar Scherer Park, Inc. Contact the president at 1843 S. Tamiami Trail, Osprey, FL 34229. To become a park volunteer contact the park manager at (941) 483-5957.

THE CARLTON RESERVE (S–45)

Location: 1800 Mabry Carlton Parkway, Venice, FL. Go north on Jacaranda Blvd. (exit 193 from I-75) to Border Road; turn east and continue 2.5 miles past Myakka River to Mabry Carlton Parkway. Entrance is .5 miles to gravel drive on right.

Phone: (941) 486-2547

Facilities: Restrooms and water are available.

Hours: Sunrise to sunset.

Highlights: The reserve borders the Myakka River and joins with Myakka State Park to the north. Four primary habitats characterize the park: wet prairie, hammock, forested wetland, and pine flatwoods. Over 130 bird species have been identified at the reserve.

The Carlton Reserve is a large tract (24,565 acres) purchased in 1982 by Sarasota County for a potable water source. A large electrodialysis reversal water treatment plant is operated by Sarasota County on the property. Only a small part of the tract (117 acres) is open to public use without a permit. Though the area open to the public without permit only contains approximately two miles of trails (the Loring Lovell Interpretive Trail), several dirt roads and trails crisscross the reserve's backcountry so access is available to all areas without bushwhacking. A map is recommended should you decide to venture into the backcountry.

The Carlton Reserve is not a popular tourist destination like Myakka State Park, but many of the same features can be enjoyed here. To enter the more interesting parts and hike along the river you must obtain a backcountry permit by calling (941) 486-2547 or (941) 316-1172. Arrangements can be made to pick up the permit at the reserve.

The Carlton Reserve has a reputation for being overrun with feral hogs. Areas uprooted by hogs can be so disturbed that they appear to be plowed. Walking these areas can be unpleasant.

Get Involved: Encourage the county parks department to issue backcountry permits by self-registration. Encourage the parks department to allow primitive camping.

JELKS TRACT (S–49)

Location: On River Road, Sarasota County west of I-75.

Facilities: Portable toilets and parking.

Highlights: A tract along the Myakka River west of I-75, this property contains a first-rate hammock along the Myakka River. Owned by Sarasota County, the tract was opened to public use without a permit in late 2002.

Myakkahatchee Environmental Park (S-46)

Location: 6968 Reisterstown Road, North Port, FL, 34287. Take I-75 exit 182 (Sumter Blvd); travel north to Tropicaire Blvd. Turn west and continue to Reisterstown Road; turn north to park entrance in approximately one mile.

Phone: (941) 486-2706

Facilities: Wheelchair accessible restrooms and water are available.

Hours: 8:00 A.M. till 10:00 P.M.

Highlights: The Myakkahatchee Creek (Big Slough) bisects the 131-acre park, which is characterized by hammock and forested wetland. Hammock canopy shades large open spaces. The wetland edges make the park a birding "hotspot."

The trails in this park are multiple use so you may share the trails with bicyclists and horseback riders. Dirt tracks parallel both sides of Myakkahatchee Creek, which are well shaded on the north side of the creek. Although the park is small, the trails connect to Oaks Park and Butler Park. The combined trail mileage is about ten miles. At times parts of the trail may be practically impassable due to high water and overgrowth. Limited trimming or maintenance is done to the trails because the park is managed to be natural. In addition to songbirds, you may see turkeys. Otters and alligators live in the creek.

Oaks Park (S-47)

Location: Mandrake Ave., North Port, FL, 34287. Take I-75 exit 182 (Sumter Blvd.) east to Lady Slipper Drive; turn north and follow Lady Slipper Dr. as it curves back east to the park entrance. The park address is Mandrake Ave., but this street is not marked.

Phone: (941) 316-1172

Facilities: None except picnic tables.

Hours: 6:00 A.M. till midnight.

Highlights: This small park (11 acres) is also bisected by Myakkahatchee Creek (Big Slough). The primary habitat is hammock. The trails are multiple use. In addition to hiking, this park is also good for off-road bicycling and is connected to Myakkahatchee Park by dirt trails that are at times overgrown or flooded and therefore barely passable.

LITTLE MANATEE RIVER STATE RECREATION AREA (N–2)

Location: 215 Lightfoot Road, Wimauma, FL, 33598. Take U.S. 301 north into Hillsborough County; turn west on Lightfoot Road and continue to park entrance on right.

Phone: (813) 671-5005

Website: www.funandsun.com/parks

Facilities: RV and primitive camping, restrooms, water. Entrance fee.

Hours: 8:00 A.M. to sunset.

Highlights: The biggest draw at Little Manatee River State Recreation Area is the superlative six-mile loop hiking trail. Although in Hillsborough County, this 2,020-acre park is included in this guide due to its first-rate hiking trail and proximity to Manatee County. The six-mile loop hiking trail parallels the Little Manatee River for several miles. Mostly shaded, this well-marked trail traverses many different habitats in a short distance. Primarily riverine habitat, you'll also walk hardwood swamp, marsh, flatwoods, scrub, pine forest, and mixed pine/hardwood forest. These varied habitats, all in close proximity, attract many different bird species. Alligators are not uncommon.

To hike the six-mile trail, you must enter the park and obtain a permit and the combination for the gate at the trail access. The trail access is north on U.S. 301 about one mile.

Although the six-mile loop trail is the best trail, several other trails and dirt roads crisscross the park on the west side of the river and are worthwhile to hike.

Lake Manatee State Recreation Area (N-11)

Location: 20007 S.R. 64, Bradenton, FL, 34202. From I-75 take State Road 64 (Exit 220A) east approximately seven miles to the entrance on the north side of the highway.

Phone: (941) 741-3028

Facilities: RV and tent camping, restrooms, water. Entrance fee.

Hours: 8:00 A.M. to sunset.

Highlights: This small park located on the shore of Lake Manatee does not have the best hiking in the area, but it is a good place for canoeing. The habitat is mostly pine flatwoods and sand pine scrub.

Myakka State Forest (S-65)

Location: From U.S. 41 go south on South River Road (State Road 777) about four miles and turn east at the forest entrance road.

Phone: (941) 480-3145 (park office)

Facilities: Toilets at parking area, no water. Maps are sometimes available at the kiosk at trailhead. The park office is at 4723 53rd Ave. East, Bradenton, FL, 34203.

Hours: Sunrise to sunset.

Highlights: The Myakka River flows through the 8,532-acre forest. The Myakkahatchee Creek also flows into the Myakka River within the forest boundaries. The forest also contains the Ainger Creek headwaters.

Acquired by the state in 1995, the Division of Forestry now manages the small forest for multiple uses—timber, wildlife, outdoor recreation, ecological restoration, and hydrological restoration. Prior to purchase by the state, the property was improved for pasture. As a result, many acres of the forest do not represent natural habitat, which must be restored. The primary habitat is pine flatwoods. Unfortunately, only a small section of forest borders the Myakka River.

Multiple-use dirt roads (biking, hiking, horseback riding, and off-road vehicles) loop through the north and south section through open pine flatwoods and along depression marshes. During wet periods, the trails are subject to flooding.

Animals and birds you may see are the bald eagle, sandhill crane, pileated woodpecker, and bobcat. Manatees are sometimes in the river.

UPPER MYAKKA RIVER WATERSHED (N–9)

Location: Travel north from Myakka City on Myakka Road. A public access point is at the intersection of Taylor Road and Myakka Road and on Myakka Road, south of Maple Creek.

Facilities: None, no parking except along highway.

Hours: Sunrise to sunset.

Highlights: The habitat at Upper Myakka River Watershed is hardwood swamp bordered by flatwoods. The headwaters of the Myakka River bisect this property. This tract owned by the Southwest Florida Water Management District is for the back-country hiker. No access is allowed except on foot at designated access points. The tract is fenced and posted with no trespassing signs, although in small print the signs allow foot traffic. Some dirt roads are passable through pine flatwoods. The more interesting hikes are in the hardwood swamps. Many hardwood trees in the swamp are dying, which some ecologists believe may be caused by drainage from agricultural lands.

You will see water snakes and wading birds in the hardwood swamp. Sandhill cranes may be seen around the swamp fringe and in depression marshes.

The Southwest Florida Water Management District had not developed an outdoor recreation plan for this tract although the district has owned the land for many years. From all appearances little has been done in that regard although the legislature had mandated that the district accommodate public recreational usage on all their lands.

Get Involved: Encourage the Water Management District to provide more appropriate signage, small parking areas, and more access points.

A recreational guide for Water Management District land can be obtained from the Southwest Florida Water Management District, Land Resources Department, 2379 Broad Street, Brooksville, FL 34604-6899. Telephone: 1-800-423-1476. Maps are also on the web at www.swfwmd.state.fl.us/recguide.

LAKE MANATEE LOWER WATERSHED (N–10)

Location: Travel east on State Road 64, the dirt road entrance is about 1.6 miles past the Myakka River Bridge. The gate will be locked. You'll walk almost a half a mile on a dirt road before you get to the tract.

Facilities: None.

Hours: No posted hours.

Highlights: The Southwest Florida Water Management District also owns this tract. Access is limited to foot traffic from the one public access point. Dirt roads crisscross the property. The Water Management District has not developed a land use plan incorporating recreational opportunities.

Canoeing and Kayaking

anatee and Sarasota Counties are located on the Gulf of Mexico. They border Tampa Bay, Sarasota Bay, Little Sarasota Bay, Blackburn Bay, and Lemon Bay, and are bisected by the Myakka, Manatee, and Braden Rivers. Studded with numerous creeks, bays, and several large lakes, you could spend weeks exploring by canoe and kayak. Except in the Gulf or the larger bays, paddling is generally easy. The river currents are moderate except during high water when they can be fast and dangerous.

Sarasota and Manatee Counties are a paddling paradise for many reasons. Most importantly, you can paddle year-round. Generally, water temperatures in the Gulf of Mexico are warm, rarely dropping below the mid-fifties and then for only a few weeks during cold winters. Except for a few days each year, fog will not limit paddling. Paddling opportunities range from novice canoeing to expert sea kayaking. Whatever your skill level, you can find a suitable location from calm lakes, streams, and bayous, to open water and breaking surf. Many different natural habitats can be observed from the water as well as human adaptations to the environment. Landscaping ranges from natural to manicured lawns. Architecture varies from skyscrapers and mansions to tract homes and rustic cabins.

Winds are usually light to calm with occasional higher winds resulting from winter cold fronts and thunderstorms. Local NOAA weather or other reliable forecasts should be checked before any paddle. (NOAA Weather Service Broadcast: telephone (813) 645-2506, WX-1 162.550 MH on VHF marine radio, automatic weather monitor (941) 388-1908.) Threatening conditions are generally forecast well in advance with the exception of summer thunderstorms, which can arise unexpectedly. Thunderstorms can be quite violent with drenching tropical rain, high winds, and lightning—the greatest danger. The Tampa Bay area has more lightning than any other area in the United States, and it often strikes miles ahead of approaching clouds. Take shelter well before a storm is overhead. The risk from staying on the water when lightning threatens should not be underestimated. Lightning killed a kayaker in Sarasota Bay in 1993. Be alert to the weather at all times and head for shelter early.

Paddling is more comfortable in winter, spring, and fall when temperatures are cooler. In summer, heat can be minimized by early morning starts. With early starts you can also avoid the afternoon thunderstorms that are common in summer.

Tides are only about two vertical feet. Tidal flow rarely prevents progress by a moderately strong paddler. In some places, like constricted passes, tidal flow can be stronger. Of course, paddling is easier with the tide. Tide charts, helpful for planning, can be obtained at tackle shops and on the Internet at www.offshoreweather.com. Major newspapers also carry tide tables.

Generally, calm water can be found for paddling even on windy days. If the Gulf of Mexico or larger bays are too rough, calm water can be found on the rivers, creeks, lakes, or small bays. Usually waves in the Gulf of Mexico are moderate and the bays have light chop. Nevertheless, conditions can change rapidly especially in the Gulf of Mexico. Know your ability to handle rough water and don't get caught in conditions beyond your skill. In some conditions, such as high winds ahead of a front, waves in the Gulf of Mexico can reach five feet or higher. Chop in bigger bays can be more than three feet. Know the predicted wave heights. You can find them on the NOAA weather forecasts.

In a subtropical environment some paddlers wrongly assume that hypothermia is not a threat. Yet more people die from hypothermia in temperatures above freezing than below freezing. Hypothermia rapidly degrades mental and physical ability, and diminished skills can cause drowning. In winter, local water temperatures in the Gulf of Mexico can drop to the mid-fifties, more than cold enough to make you susceptible to hypothermia if you capsize. Likewise, if you get wet from spray, rain, or fog, wind chill can easily drop your body temperature into the danger zone even on mild days. Prepare and dress for anticipated conditions.

Minimum recommended equipment for open canoes is a compass, NOAA marine charts for coastal navigation (#11425, Charlotte Harbor to Tampa Bay, and #11417, South Tampa Bay), a personal flotation device (PFD), a Coast Guard–approved noisemaker, a bailer, a sponge, an extra paddle, bow and stern lines, a flashlight, a first aid kit, a survival knife, an anchor with sufficient line, and USCG–approved visual distress signals (orange distress flag, electric, and pyrotechnic). Note that USCG pyrotechnic distress signals (flares) are required for night paddling. Kayakers, in addition, should have pumps, paddle floats, and spray skirts. Canoeists should consider a VHF radio. Kayakers need a radio and should keep it handy, not out of reach in a compartment. Cellular telephones can be used for emergency communication, but cellular phones do not substitute for a VHF radio.

Safety should always be your first priority. Wear your PFD. Know how to swim, self-rescue, and buddy-rescue. Do not paddle at night without proper Coast Guard–approved navigational lighting and visual signaling devices. Do not paddle without knowing local conditions. For example, know water levels. Flooded streams can be dangerous and low-water creeks and bayous can be impassable. Know how to handle your equipment. Local outfitters can teach you the basics or upgrade your skill level.

Don't paddle barefoot; wear booties or sandals to protect your feet. Although they might not look dangerous, oyster and pen shells have cut many paddlers. Don't be foolish and walk or scrape against them—they can cut like razor blades.

Don't paddle the Intracoastal Waterways and marked channels in the passes except to cross. Boat traffic can be heavy and fast there. When you cross, cross quickly and cross perpendicular to the channel where practical.

Always paddle with drinking water within reach. Paddlers

have been known to have water in their boat but are unable to get to it. Don't aggravate yourself unnecessarily with that mistake. Drink before you're thirsty. Because you are often cool when paddling you can become dehydrated without realizing it. Do not paddle in designated swimming areas or prohibited areas like dam outfalls.

This guide intentionally does not route specific canoe or kayak trails. This guide suggests areas to paddle with general information to plan your own trip without necessarily following a designated trail. In some respects designated trails detract from a primary advantage that canoes and kayaks provide. With small boats, you can poke around off trail into remote, almost inaccessible areas. So use this guide in conjunction with your navigation charts to plan your trips. The guide provides the generalities. The charts provide the details.

The paddling areas listed in this booklet center around launch sites. Generally, the launches are organized from north to south and by major water body. Many good paddles in the book may loop back to the starting place. Primary and alternative launch sites are listed so different routes can be paddled and shuttles arranged. For instance, a strong sea kayaker could launch at Holmes Beach and paddle south in the Gulf of Mexico for takeout at North Shell Road, Siesta Key.

Nevertheless, for beginners or for those who simply prefer trails; good trails do exist. For example, Ft. Desoto Park, Cockroach Bay, Lido Key, and Myakkahatchee Creek have designated trails. Manatee County has several marked trails with more under development. Manatee County's Guide to Area Canoe and Kayak Trails is excellent. Sources for trail maps are listed in the resource section in this booklet. Sometimes trail maps are available at the trailheads, but always have a chart and compass as all the trail markers on the maps may not exist. All markers may not be in place as marked, and trail markers sometimes get destroyed or vandalized. More importantly, you may want to leave the trail for your own adventure.

LITTLE MANATEE RIVER STATE RECREATION AREA

Location: 215 Lightfoot Road, Wimauma, FL, 33598. Take U.S. 41 north into Hillsborough County; turn west on Lightfoot Road and continue to park entrance.

Phone: (813) 671-5005

Website: www.funandsun/parks

Launch: Boat ramp off the park entrance road.

Facilities: RV and tent camping. Restrooms and water. Entrance fee.

Hours: 8:00 A.M. to sunset

Highlights: The Little Manatee River flowing through this park is designated as an Outstanding Florida Water and is part of the Cockroach Bay Aquatic Preserve.

The Little Manatee River flows through the park for five miles. Exceptionally scenic, the topography along the river varies from swampy to high sandy banks. At the park, water levels will rise and fall with the tide. The habitats along the river comprise hardwood forests, swamps, pine flatwoods, scrub, willow marsh, and riverine. You may see any wild mammal found in Florida except black bear or panther. Bird watching is excellent due to the variety of habitats.

UPPER MANATEE RIVER

RYE WILDERNESS PARK N-12

Location: Rye Wilderness Park, 905 Rye Road off State Road 64, Parrish, FL. From I-75, travel east on State Road 64 to Upper Manatee River Road; turn north and follow Upper Manatee River to the intersection with Rye Road.

Phone: (941) 776-0900

Launch: Less than 100 yards west of Rye Road on Upper Manatee River Road.

Facilities: None except off-road parking at Rye Road canoe/skiff launch. Water and restrooms at Rye Wilderness Park, main entrance, northeast across the river toward the Sheriff's Youth Ranch.

Hours: Sunrise to sunset.

Highlights: This stretch of the Manatee River is a designated Florida Greenways and Trails System canoe trail. During moderate to low water this route can be paddled both ways so that no shuttle is needed. The paddle from Rye Bridge upstream to the Lake Manatee Dam is about 3.5 miles. Water levels may vary from water releases from the Lake Manatee dam. Maintain a safe distance from the dam. Do not go beyond the warning signs. A siren sounds when water is released from the dam. Be alert, waves generated by the release can capsize a small boat.

GAMBLE CREEK AND MANATEE RIVER RESORT (N–13)

Location: From I-75 go east on State Road 64. In about two miles turn north on Upper Manatee River Road; continue slightly over two miles to Mill Creek Road; turn left (north) on Mill Creek Road and continue to Manatee River Resort.

Phone: (941) 749-1146

Launch: Manatee River Resort (Private). Call ahead to verify operating hours.

Facilities: Private boat ramp. Fees are charged for launch. Rental equipment may be available.

Hours: Call to verify.

Alternative launch: Ft. Hamer Road Park at the southern terminus of Ft. Hamer Road on the north side of the river. Paddle upstream to explore the Gamble Creek area.

Alternative launch: Ray's Canoe Hideaway and Kayak Center (Private): 1247 Hagle Park Road, Bradenton. From I-75 take State Road 64 to Upper Manatee River Road; turn north and continue on Upper Manatee River Road to Hagle Road; turn north and continue to Ray's. Call ahead to verify operating times: (941) 474-3909.

Highlights: This is an excellent area to explore, with its many dead-end sloughs and scenic creeks. You can explore both salt marsh and freshwater marsh habitats. In this area, the maze-like creeks keep paddling interesting, and you will backtrack as you explore. Look for several "hidden" channels on the north side of the river that open into bayous. Vultures roost in the area.

LAKE MANATEE RECREATION AREA (N–11)

Location: 20007 S.R. 64, Bradenton, FL 34202. From I-75 take State Road 64 east approximately seven miles to the entrance on the north side of the highway.

Phone: (941) 741-3028

Facilities: RV camping/tent camping. Entrance fee.

Launch: Boat ramp.

Hours: 8:00 A.M. to sunset.

Highlights: Lake paddle on a nine-mile-long reservoir. Several creeks, both on the north and south side of the reservoir, can be explored. The lake has good fishing for bass and pan fish.

This recreation area has only 556 acres, but it extends three miles along the south shore of Lake Manatee reservoir. The primary habitats are pine flatwoods with some depression marshes, sand pine scrub, and hammock. Bobcats are sometimes sighted along with the occasional deer.

UPPER BRADEN RIVER

JIGG'S LANDING (N–16)

Location: From I-75 take State Road 70 west; turn south at Braden River Road; continue about one mile to Jigg's Landing fish camp.

Phone: (941) 756-6745

Launch: Boat ramp (private with fee).

Facilities: Jigg's Landing is a fish camp. Restrooms, bait, and small stores are available.

Hours: No posted hours.

Alternative Launch: State Road 64 Boat Ramp. From I-75, travel west on State Road 64. The ramp is just beyond the Braden River

Bridge on the south side of S.R. 64. Just upstream you can circumnavigate many little islands. Watch your tide tables; some routes can be impassable at low water.

Alternative Launch: Braden River Park. 10850 State Road 70, Bradenton. Take State Road 70 west from I-75 to 51st Street, which is just west from the Braden River Bridge. Turn north on 51st Street. At publication this ramp was not open but is projected for 2003.

Highlights: From Jigg's Landing, you can take a beautiful river paddle upstream to high sand banks or paddle the Bill Evers Reservoir.

For the first several miles upstream from Jigg's Landing, the Braden River shoreline is developed. Farther upstream development thins and powerboat traffic decreases due to the sandbars at low water. The Braden River is one of the better streams for fly-fishing in the area. You cannot portage the Braden River Dam. To paddle above the dam, launch at Jigg's Landing.

TAMPA BAY

Notice: Pay close attention to the weather forecast, winds, tides, and currents when paddling in or near Tampa Bay or the Gulf of Mexico. Conditions can change rapidly and dramatically, particularly in open water.

COCKROACH BAY (N-1)

Location: Travel north on U.S. 41 into Hillsborough County, turn west on Cockroach Bay Road, continue west to the boat ramp at Cockroach Bay.

Launch: Boat ramp with suggested donation.

Facilities: None except parking. Maps are sometimes available at the kiosk on site.

Hours: No posted hours.

Highlights: Cockroach Bay is an aquatic preserve with high quality mangrove bayous with marked canoe trails. It is located about two miles north of Manatee County but is included in this guide due to its proximity and quality habitat. Cockroach Bay can be fairly described as a premier mangrove bayou habitat. Two marked canoe trails (Snook Canoe Trail to the north, and Horseshoe Crab Canoe Trail to the south) start and end at the boat ramp. Bring your own chart. The paddle is easiest at high tide since the trails are shallow at low tide. The trails meander through mangrove channels, which are protected from moderate winds.

Not named for the cockroach, Cockroach Bay is named for the horseshoe crabs, called "cockroaches of the sea" by Spanish explorers. Roseate spoonbills roost in the bayous. White pelicans and flocks of ducks are commonly seen in winter and East Indian manatees enter the bayous. Look for the osprey nests along Cockroach Bay Road.

Hillsborough County Parks and Recreation Department maintains a large nature preserve near the boat ramp, which is accessible by foot during daylight hours.

ADDITIONAL INFORMATION:
Tampa Bay Watch, Inc.
8401 Ninth St. North, Suite 230-B
St. Petersburg, FL 33702
Telephone: (727) 896-5320
www.tampabaywatch.org
info@tampabaywatch.org

Hillsborough County Parks and Recreation
1102 East River Cove Drive
Tampa, FL 33604
Telephone: (863) 975-2160
www.hillsboroughcounty.org/parks/home

SUNSHINE SKYWAY/BISHOP HARBOR (N-3)
Location: From US-41, north of Bradenton turn West on Bishop Harbor Rd. (St. Rd. 683). In about a mile, look for the canoe/kayak launch on the right.
Launch: About a mile down Bishop Harbor Road.

Facilities: None.

Hours: No posted hours at the boat ramp.

Alternative Launch: A little further west down Bishop Harbor Road at the boat ramp on the north side of the road.

Alternative Launch: Sunshine Skyway: exit I-275 at the rest area at the south end of the Sunshine Skyway. To launch you will have to lift your boat over barricades at the south end of the parking area.

Highlights: Bishop Harbor offers good paddling and good views of the Sunshine Skyway Bridge. Exit the harbor to the south to paddle around mangrove islands in Tampa Bay.

Bishop Harbor has grass flats and mangrove thickets along the north shore. The Manatee County Terra Ceia Paddling Trail loops into Bishop Harbor, (3 miles for the Harbor circumnavigation). Exploring the Mangrove barrier islands and the inlets between the Sunshine Skyway and Bishop Harbor can extend the paddle. Ospreys are commonly sighted.

The Southwest Water Management District owns property along the harbor, which is accessible by foot only.

EMERSON POINT/MIGUEL BAY/TERRA CEIA BAY (N-7)
Location: 5801 17th St. West, Palmetto. From U.S. 41 turn west on 10th Street in Palmetto and follow signs to Emerson Point.

Phone: (941) 776-2295 or 742-5923

Launch: Beach launch at end of the park road.

Facilities: Portable toilets at park entrance. Facilities are being upgraded.

Hours: Daylight to sunset.

Alternative Launch: Warner's Bayou Park Boat Ramp at 58th St. and Riverview Blvd., Bradenton, on the south bank of the Manatee River. Beach launch is possible. The ramp area can be crowded. No restrooms or water. No posted hours.

Alternative Launch: Crab Trap Boat Ramp, U.S. 19 north of Palmetto on the west side of the causeway, provides access to the east end of Terra Ceia Bay.

Highlights: Circumnavigate Snead Island and Rattlesnake Key to enjoy barrier island geography and excellent views of the Sunshine Skyway Bridge.

Paddle to Miguel Bay along mangrove fringe and red mangrove with excellent views of the the bridge. Rattlesnake Key can be circumnavigated although the unmarked route on the east side is moderately difficult to find. A little tidal creek, navigable at high tide, winds through Rattlesnake Key. Miguel Bay is a good location for tidal pond studies because marine organisms are often visible in the shallow water. Rays, soft corals, and horseshoe crabs are common. A sandy beach suitable for a rest stop is at the northeast tip of Rattlesnake Key.

Manatee County's Terra Ceia Paddling Trail skirts the north side of Emerson Point. Expect to see ducks and common loons in winter. Chop is often quite rough at the crossing from Emerson Point to Rattlesnake Key, particularly when the tide runs against the wind.

A circumnavigation of Snead Island is another alternative paddle from Emerson Point. Snead Island is largely developed, but Emerson Point Park (195 acres) at the west end is pristine. A tower near the entrance provides a terrific view of the topography of Tampa Bay and mangrove forests. A big Indian mound, where early settlers built a home, is just inside the park entrance. Although the home burned, a concrete cistern and foundation remnants remain.

The Indian mound, like most in Florida, has no connection to tribes presently living in Florida. Indigenous Native Americans in Florida had been exterminated by disease, war, and slavery by the time of the American Revolution. The Seminoles— a mixture of Creeks, other indigenous peoples, and escaped slaves—moved into Florida later to escape American efforts to remove them to reservations in the west. The Indian mound, accessible from the water, is located just west of the Bradenton Yacht Club on the south shore. Look for the royal palm trees and an opening in the mangroves.

Dramatic bird life can be seen at Emerson Point. Roseate spoonbills are sometimes visible and wood storks are not uncommon. From the tower a bird roost can be seen on the northwest shore.

Fishing is excellent along the mangrove shore and grass flats on the north side of the island. Terra Ceia Bay is designated as a State Aquatic Preserve and Outstanding Florida Water.

The Snead Island cut-off between Terra Ceia Bay and the Manatee River sometimes has heavy boat and personal watercraft traffic. While the Manatee River does have a designated boat channel, powerboats often cruise outside the channel. Stay close to shore to avoid the worst powerboat traffic.

For an interesting historical and natural history exploration, cross the Manatee River to Desoto Point and Riverview Pointe Park. Hernando de Soto may have landed near here to begin his gold-seeking exploration in 1539. His six-hundred-man Spanish army tramped around the Southeast without ever finding significant gold. A small museum at the DeSoto National Memorial at the point tells the history.

Adjacent to Desoto Point, Riverview Pointe Park has many different habitats squeezed into a very small area. Within a short stroll, you can walk from sea level mangrove and beach habitat up the riverbank to oak/hickory hammock that transitions to sand pine scrub. You cannot find a better place to study various habitats in a small area.

Remember, crossing the Manatee River from Emerson Point to Desoto Point can be dangerous due to current, waves, and heavy powerboat traffic. In short, do not attempt this route in an open boat. Have experience and use a spray skirt for this paddle.

ANNA MARIA/EGMONT KEY N–6

Location: Egmont Key is an island at the mouth of Tampa Bay only accessible by boat.

Website: http://egmontkey.fws.gov/

Launch: Bay Front Park, 310 North Bay Blvd., Anna Maria.

Facilities: Restrooms, but no water at Egmont Key. Restrooms, water, and showers at Bay Front Park.

Hours: 6:00 A.M. to 10:00 P.M. Overnight parking should be available at Anna Maria City Pier at the intersection of Bay Blvd. and Pine Ave., just south of Bay Front Park. Check with concessionaire.

Highlights: This paddle to a National Wildlife Refuge is probably the most challenging along this section of coast.

Egmont Key is a 350-acre island located at the mouth of Tampa Bay between Manatee and Pinellas Counties. This paddle ranks as premier, but difficult, requiring strength and skill. Except during the calmest conditions, expect to be tested. You will probably encounter breaking surf somewhere on the route. Currents can be strong. Small boat traffic can be heavy, worse if you cross a ship channel. Do not attempt this paddle by canoe or open boat. Kayak this route only if you are skilled and experienced. Remember that ships move faster than they appear to travel and that a kayak is often invisible from a ship.

This paddle provides an overview of Tampa Bay and the Sunshine Skyway Bridge. Before reaching Egmont Key you will pass Passage Key, a small island also designated as a National Wildlife Refuge. During the winter you may see migrating seabirds like gannets. A frigate bird could soar overhead or a peregrine falcon could fly by. Large sharks are common around the island even in the shallows. Greater Tampa Bay is a shark nursery and large sharks are sometimes seen near Egmont Key. Be on the lookout for the endangered East Indian manatee.

Passage Key has an interesting history. Hernando DeSoto made his first New World landing nearby and Ponce de Leon may have refilled his water casks on the island. During the Second Seminole War, settlers fled to Passage Key for refuge from the Indians and were protected there by two United States gunboats. In 1905, President Theodore Roosevelt designated Passage Key as a migratory bird refuge and the Audubon Society stationed a warden there. Historically, the Key had large trees and a spring-fed lake. The Key totally disappeared due to a hurricane storm surge in October 1921. Over the years, the Key has gradually re-emerged from the water and is now growing again.

Egmont Key was designated in 1994 as a National Wildlife Refuge, primarily to provide nesting and feeding habitat for the brown pelican. The refuge is co-managed by the U.S. Fish and Wildlife Service and Florida Park Service. The park can be contacted by phone at (727) 893-2627 or on VHF channels 16 or 80.

Ft. Dade was built on Egmont Key prior to the Spanish American War to protect Tampa Bay. The fort was deactivated in

1923 and is now washing away as the Gulf of Mexico erodes the beach. Two coast artillery batteries still exist, but others are only ruins. Although rebuilt and moved back from the beach in 1857, the lighthouse on the island was built in 1848 and is one of the oldest buildings in the Tampa Bay area

Although it is a national wildlife refuge, you can neverthe-less land on the beach. The beach is popular with powerboaters who at times crowd the beach on weekends and holidays. Gopher tortoises live on the island, along with diamondback rattlesnakes.

Should you want a longer paddle, you can cross another ship channel, the Egmont Channel, north of Egmont Key and go to Ft. Desoto Park on Mullet Key. A Pinellas County Park, Ft. Desoto Park also has an abandoned fort built before the Spanish American War. The fort still contains a battery of twelve-inch mortars and two 1890 rapid-fire canons.

Ft. Desoto is an Audubon birding hotspot. During the spring and fall migrations, you may see birds like painted buntings, which are uncommon in most local areas. Expect to see the more common pelicans, cormorants, herons, and black skimmers. The park head-quarters has timely information about the best birding hotspots.

Ft. Desoto Park consists of five interconnected islands totaling nine hundred acres. There's a 2.25-mile canoe trail. Facilities include both RV and tent camping, plus twenty restroom buildings and concessions/snack bars.

You can avoid an open water crossing and still explore Ft. Desoto Park and Mullet Key Bayou by driving to Ft. Desoto Park. The park is located at 3500 Pinellas Bayways, Tierra Verde, FL, 33715, and can be reached by telephone at (727) 866-2484. The website is http://fortdesoto.com

GULF OF MEXICO

HOLMES BEACH (N–19)

Location: Intersection of Manatee Ave. and Gulf Drive, Holmes Beach.

Launch: Beach launch to Gulf of Mexico. At the south end of the public beach there is public beach access. Do not launch in the swimming area.

Facilities: Restrooms, water, outdoor showers, café, and parking at Holmes Beach.

Hours: Dawn to 10:00 P.M.

Highlights: This is probably the first practical launch site on the Gulf of Mexico traveling south from the tip of Anna Maria Island. Although there are other small beach access points farther north, they entail a portage, have limited or no parking, and close at sunset. Be sure to look for the monk parakeets nesting in the sabal palms near the cafe.

PALMA SOLA BAY

PERICO ISLAND (N–18)

Location: Northwest Bradenton, accessed from the Palma Sola Causeway.

Launch: Palma Sola Causeway, take State Road 64 (Manatee Ave.) west until you reach the causeway. Look for appropriate launch along causeway.

Facilities: Several convenience stores and gas stations are east of the causeway.

Hours: No posted hours.

Highlights: Perico Island, a Manatee County Blue Water Trail, is a compact area with paddling variety. It can be circumnavigated by traveling southwest from the causeway then bearing north into Perico Bayou. Stay close to shore because boat traffic can be heavy and personal watercraft can be a nuisance. You should be able to find areas with calm water and little boat traffic because numerous small island and inlets are scattered around Perico Island. Mangrove thickets, oyster beds, and sea grass beds make this an excellent area for fishing and bird watching.

Note that when you exit Perico Bayou to the north, you are exposed to open water and heavy boat traffic. Open boats should proceed with caution or backtrack. The prettiest areas are in the more protected waters in Perico Bayou and at the southern end of Perico Island.

An alternative paddle is along the shoreline of Palma Sola Bay. Mangroves and sea grass beds line the southeast shore. Unfortunately, no long creeks enter Palma Sola Bay.

SARASOTA BAY

LEFFIS KEY (N–20)

Location: About a half mile north from Longboat Pass on the east side of Gulf of Mexico Drive at Coquina Park.

Launch: South Coquina Boat Ramp or beach launch at the southeast end of Bradenton Beach (north side of Longboat Pass) or North Coquina Boat Ramp just north from Leffis Key.

Facilities: Restrooms, water, and telephone.

Hours: 6:00 A.M. to midnight.

Highlights: Leffis Key is a small island separated by a narrow canal from Bradenton Beach. Personal watercraft and other power-boat traffic can be heavy especially on weekends and holidays.

Leffis Key was severely degraded with spoil when the Intracoastal Waterway was dug. The area was restored under the auspices of the National Estuary Program by excavating tidal lagoons and creating tidal wetlands. Exotic plants were removed and native plants and grasses replanted. Spoil mounds replicate coastal ridges. The job was done so well it almost looks natural. An excellent boardwalk with terrific views meanders around the key and along Sarasota Bay. The Audubon Society describes the area around Longboat Pass as a birding hot spot. Over thirty-five species of warbler and more than two hundred species overall have been seen in this area. At any time of year, you will see common wading birds. Of course, during migrations more birds will be seen. Should you be lucky, you'll spot a reddish egret. The bird is easily identified by its unusual feeding behavior. Spreading its wings, it will run through shallow water stabbing at fish confused by the shadow from its wings.

Get Involved: Join and support the Audubon Society. Not just for birding, the Audubon Society is a premier conservation and environmental organization with a long history of protecting the environment. The Audubon Society has been instrumental in preserving the Everglades. The society hired the first Everglades ranger, Guy Bradley, who, while protecting bird rookeries, was murdered by plume hunters.

The Sarasota Audubon Society can be contacted on the Internet at http://home.earthlink.net/ ~ sarasotaaudubon/ or at P.O. Box, 15423, Sarasota, FL, 34277-1423.

SISTER KEYS (N–23)

Location: From Gulf of Mexico Drive on Longboat Key, turn east on Broadway. At Bayside turn south to the Linely Street boat ramp.

Launch: The Linely Street boat ramp or beach launch.

Facilities: Limited parking, no restrooms or water at the Linely Street boat ramp. Two restaurants are nearby.

Hours: No posted hours at the Linely Street boat ramp.

Alternative Launch: You could paddle north along the shoreline about four miles to Palma Sola Causeway. There are numerous places to land and launch along the causeway. Manatee County maintains the Kingfish Boat Ramp where Manatee Ave. (St. Rd. 64) meets Anna Maria Island.

Alternative Launch: A Longboat Key bay access point for take-out is about six miles south from Longboat Pass in the 3400 block of Gulf of Mexico Drive, across the street from the Longview Dr. Beach Access. This access has no facilities and limited parking.

Alternative Launch: Another possible take-out is about five miles south at Bay Front Recreation Center, 4052 Gulf of Mexico Drive, Longboat Key. This launch site is marginal because it requires portage and launch over a sea wall. The hours are dawn to 10 P.M. Water is available from a fountain at the tennis courts.

Highlights: Just east across the harbor from the launch, the Sister Keys are the largest open water islands between Tampa Bay and Charlotte Harbor. Large grass flats lie to the south and east of these islands. Boat traffic can be heavy and fast in the Intracoastal Waterway. A sandbar on the north end of the Sister Keys is used for picnicking and swimming. You can extend the paddle by circumnavigating Jewfish Key north from the Sister Keys. Be alert to the tidal currents near Longboat Pass. Also, watch for personal watercraft, which are very popular in this area.

An alternative paddle is south along the shoreline of Longboat Key. Along the frequent finger canals, you can see many architectural styles common to this area. Durante Park, about three miles south, is a good destination. This City of Longboat Key Park lies northwest of Intracoastal Channel Marker 27 and has a small area where a boat can be landed. Restrooms and a water fountain are near the playground—walk west on the park path about two hundred yards.

SOUTHERN TIP OF LONGBOAT KEY
QUICK POINT NATURE PRESERVE

Location: South end of Longboat Key. Enter on the west side of Gulf of Mexico Drive just across the north end of the New Pass Bridge.

Launch: Beach launch into the bayou on the west side of New Pass.

Facilities: Limited parking, no restrooms or water. Restaurants nearby and across the pass.

Hours: 5:00 A.M. to 11:00 P.M.

Alternative launch: Bay access, 3400 block of Longboat Key, across Gulf of Mexico Drive from the Longview Drive Beach Access.

Highlights: On the east side of New Pass Bridge at Quick Point a little canal meanders through Quick Point Nature Preserve (34 acres) and exits into Sarasota Bay.

Pay attention to the tidal currents at New Pass especially near the bridge. Boat traffic can be heavy in the pass. High tide is the best time to paddle the canal through the Quick Point Nature Preserve. The circumnavigation around the park and return to the launch site should take only about an hour.

Fiddler crabs are common in this area. They are an indicator of good water quality and were once common all along the

Sarasota Bay shoreline. After this short paddle you can visit Mote Marine Laboratory just across the pass on City Island. Mote Marine has an excellent aquarium and marine exhibits, which are open to the public for a fee. In addition to its scientific research, Mote Marine is noted for excellence in environmental education.

An alternative is to paddle north along the shoreline of Longboat Key. Numerous dead end finger canals along Country Club Shores represent the way Florida waterfront developed before the detrimental environmental impact from this type development was well understood. Notice how the sea-walled canals have altered the shoreline by destroying the mangroves and the tidal transition zone. At the north end of the finger canals just before entering the Yacht Club Marina, you find a little mangrove-lined canal that will continue north and exit near Bishop's Point.

Another alternative for kayakers is to exit New Pass to the Gulf of Mexico and paddle north along Longboat Key, or paddle south along Lido Key.

Get Involved: Support Mote Marine Laboratory by visiting and becoming a member. The laboratory undertakes research on the marine environment, fisheries enhancement, and dolphin rescue to name a few areas of Mote expertise. A big shark tank highlights the Mote Aquarium. Mote Marine Laboratory is located at 1600 Ken Thompson Parkway, Sarasota, FL, 34236. The phone number is (941) 388-2451.

Injured or distressed wildlife can be reported to Pelican Man's Bird Sanctuary, 1708 Ken Thompson Parkway, Sarasota, FL, 34236. The phone number is (941) 388-4444.

ISLAND PARK (N–29)
Location: U.S. 41 and Main St., Sarasota.
Launch: Beach launch at Island Park.
Facilities: Restrooms and water, O'Leary's and Marina Jack's restaurants.
Hours: No posted hours.
Alternative Launch: Centennial Park, 10th St. and U.S. 41,

boat ramps and beach launch. Toilets and large parking lot are available on site. By using this launch you can avoid the Ringling Causeway Bridge and boat traffic around Island Park. A water fountain and restrooms are a quarter-mile north at Whitaker-Gateway Park. There are no posted hours.

Highlights: Enjoy terrific views of the city of Sarasota and the many vessels anchored in the anchorage south of Island Park.

Paddle south along the shore to see Marie Selby Botanical Gardens at the entrance to Hudson Bayou. Siesta Key Bridge is about two miles south. A large mud flat northeast from the bridge attracts wading birds and gulls.

Paddle north about five miles along the shore to see the Ringling Museum, Cà d'Zan (John Ringling's mansion), and New College of Florida.

SUN CIRCLE PARK (N–27)

Location: From U.S. 41 turn west on Indian Beach Road and continue to Bayshore Road. Take Bayshore Road north to South Shore Drive, turn west on South Shore Drive; at Sun Circle turn north and continue to the park.

Launch: Small beach launch at south end of park.

Facilities: None, street parking only.

Hours: 6:00 A.M. to 11:00 P.M.

Highlights: Sun Circle Park is a small neighborhood park by Stephen's Point. This park is only about one mile south of Cà d'Zan. Beyond Cà d'Zan you can paddle approximately three miles north to Bowless Creek.

LIDO KEY (N–34) (N–33)

Location: South Lido Park, 2201 Ben Franklin Dr., Sarasota, FL.

Launch: Canoe trail launch at the end of Taft Drive.

Facilities: Water and restrooms are available at the South Lido Park. Canoe trail maps are sometimes available at the park.

Hours: 6:00 A.M. to midnight.

Alternative Launch: Sites near Lido Key are at Bird Key Park on the John Ringling Causeway, (No restrooms, ample parking), North Shell road on Siesta Key (No restrooms and limited parking, hours: 6:00 A.M. to midnight), and Ken Thompson Park/City Island, 1700 Ken Thompson Pkwy. Lido Key, (boat ramps on the south side of City Island, restrooms).

Highlights: Suitable paddles through mangrove tidal swamp with tunnels through mangrove trees can be found for the novice canoeist or the experienced kayaker. For the novice paddler, South Lido Park has a well-marked canoe trail. You can get up close to the red mangrove trees and their prop roots. You may see a snake or raccoon among the roots. The trail follows old mosquito control ditches overgrown by mangrove trees and across Big Grassy Lagoon and Brushy Bayou. Expect to see water birds like great egrets, great blue herons, little blue herons, snowy egrets, cormorants, and pelicans. When the water is clear you can see marine animals like mud crabs and sponges. There are grass flats on the east side of South Lido Park where fishing is good. The canoe trail can be difficult to paddle at low tide and "no-see-ums" can be unpleasant during warm weather.

Extend the paddle by circumnavigating Otter Key, which is an undeveloped small mangrove island (30 acres) just southeast of St. Armands Key. Only a short stretch of open water (approximately a half mile) separates the marked canoe trail from Otter Key. Fishing is good along the mangroves and grass flats.

Experienced kayakers can circumnavigate Lido Key. This trip is about 7 1/2 miles and can take three or four hours depending on wind and tide. The circumnavigation is an excellent paddle for variety—surf in the Gulf of Mexico, tidal currents near the passes, and calm in bayous. Current in the passes can be five or more knots depending upon the tide. Do not attempt this paddle without a favorable weather forecast. Be alert to boat traffic, which can be heavy around the passes. You may see dolphins early in the morning or evening as they are often active around the passes then. You can rest or picnic at the southern tip of Longboat Key or at North Lido Park at the north end of Lido Key.

Get Involved: Since territorial days, Florida law has provided for public access to the shoreline up to the mean high water line, which is often demarcated as the wet sand area along the shore. As a consequence, you have the right to land your boat on the shore between ordinary high and ordinary low water. However, be aware that boaters who have legally come to shore have occasionally been harassed and threatened with trespass by people unfamiliar with Florida law. Likewise, law enforcement personnel may not know the law. If you are harassed, do not become confrontational with those who are uninformed. Report the circumstances to the appropriate authorities later. Cooperate with law enforcement at all times, and don't enter, or cross, private property without permission.

Unfortunately, recent legislatures, lobbied by timber and mining interests, have attempted to limit your right of access to the shoreline only to the mean low water line. If changed from the mean high water line, you will no longer have access to the shoreline except where the property is publicly owned. In the 2000 legislative session, the change lost by only one vote in the Florida Senate. Inform yourself on this issue and notify your representative, senator, and the governor that your right to the shoreline for public use and enjoyment should not be limited.

NORTH SHELL ROAD, SIESTA KEY

Location: Siesta Key, Sarasota, Florida. Turn west from Higel Ave. onto North Shell Road, continue straight ahead to unpaved parking area.

Launch: Beach launch where Shell Road meets Big Sarasota Pass.

Facilities: None; limited parking.

Hours: 6:00 A.M. to midnight.

Highlights: For experienced kayakers there is often breaking surf along the sandbar at the mouth of the Big Pass.

This is an excellent launch for experienced kayakers wishing to explore the Big Sarasota Pass area. South Lido Park is north across the pass about one-half mile. Big Sarasota Pass is an excellent place to see dolphins especially around sunrise. Powerboat traffic and personal watercraft can be heavy especially on weekends and holidays.

Another good paddle from this launch is north around the northern tip of Siesta Key then south into Hanson Bayou and east to Roberts Bay. People sometimes camp at Big Edwards Island near the Intracoastal Waterway or at Skiers Island further south. A bird rookery is just east across the Intracoastal from Little Edwards Island.

LITTLE SARASOTA BAY

JIM NEVILLE PRESERVE AND MIDNIGHT PASS (S–38)

Location: Southern tip of Siesta Key reached by going south on Midnight Pass road to Turtle Beach Park, a Sarasota County Park.

Launch: Public boat ramp across the street from the beach at Turtle Beach Park, Siesta Key.

Facilities: Both water and restrooms are available. Midnight Pass Pub is across the street from the park. Parking is available away from the boat ramp, which is limited to vehicles with trailers.

Hours: 6:00 A.M. to midnight.

Alternative Launch: Osprey Fishing Pier at the end of Main St. in Osprey. No restrooms or water and limited parking. The launch site is an old boat ramp that has a low chain across it. On the mainland, this site is about a half-mile directly east across Roberts Bay from the Jim Neville Preserve and the Bird Keys.

Highlights: Nearby mangrove islands, spoil islands, the Jim Neville Preserve, and Midnight Pass estuary are all easily accessible from the launch. The lagoon at Turtle Beach Park is very protected and a good place to practice paddling skills. Fishing is good at the grass flats just east of Siesta Key.

In about three hours, the Jim Neville Preserve, Midnight Pass estuary, Palmer Point, and the Bird Keys east of Siesta Key can be circumnavigated with launch and take-out at Turtle Beach Park boat ramp, in the sheltered bay. This area is generally protected from the wind and fast boat traffic except near the Intracoastal Waterway. The lagoon at Turtle Beach Public Park opens into Little Sarasota Bay near the former Midnight Pass. Here, you can observe an area modified by the hotly contested political decision closing Midnight Pass to the Gulf of Mexico.

Like many passes along the Gulf of Mexico, Midnight Pass migrated up and down the beach. In 1984 it migrated so far north that private residences were at risk of washing away. The Sarasota County Commission voted to close the active pass and dig a new pass approximately a quarter mile south. The "new pass" only stayed open a short time before it filled with sand. Afterward, permits could not be obtained to re-open the pass without engineering and biological studies. The longer the pass stayed closed the greater public furor grew. "Self-help" volunteers brought their shovels in an unsuccessful effort to open the pass. The controversy still rages. Many in the community want the pass opened. Those favoring a re-opened pass argue that Little Sarasota Bay needs the flushing action from an open pass and that the bay is more polluted since the pass closed. Those favoring an open pass also want boat access between Little Sarasota Bay and the Gulf of Mexico restored. Many cars in Sarasota County still have bumper stickers that read "Midnight Pass, Let It Flow."

On the other hand, some argue that Little Sarasota Bay in the Midnight Pass area is now a more productive fishery than before the pass was closed. They argue the pass closing has not been deleterious to the environment. For example, they point out that grass flats have expanded in the area since closure. Those opposed to opening the pass also argue that the pass would only close again or migrate if opened. They argue that maintaining an open pass would require constant dredging or jetties and cost millions.

Paddle around and observe. Contrast the Midnight Pass environment with an open pass like Venice Inlet, New Pass, or Stump Pass.

The Bird Keys were built up by material taken from the Intracoastal Waterway when it was dug. These spoil islands have extensive stands of exotic Australian pines that crowd out and kill native vegetation. Until cleared by county personnel and volunteers, Palmer Point at the south side of the pass was also covered with Australian pines and other exotics. Notice how native vegetation is returning and is already more diverse than the

Australian pine monoculture found on the Bird Keys.

Poking around at high tide, you can find little gaps and tunnels through the mangroves to tidal ponds. Roseate spoonbills have been seen in these ponds. Reddish egrets are also attracted to the tidal flats. The grass flats between Siesta Key and the Bird Keys are good fishing for spotted sea trout and redfish.

As you leave the lagoon and head south around the point toward Midnight Pass, you can see an old concrete pool and crumbled concrete walls. These were used as shark pens when Mote Marine Laboratory was on Siesta Key.

Experienced paddlers can cross Little Sarasota Bay to the bayou that leads to Catfish Creek and North Creek. Be patient, the entrance to the creeks is small and not easy to find. High-rise condos now loom over what was once an exceptionally beautiful paddle.

Get Involved: Inform yourself about the Midnight Pass controversy. Volunteer to remove Australian Pines and other exotics on Palmer Point and the spoil islands. Encourage the County Parks Department to provide better access for canoe and kayak launch at Osprey Fishing Pier.

BLACKBURN BAY

OSCAR SCHERER STATE PARK AND SOUTH CREEK (N-42)

Location: 1843 S. Tamiami Trail, Osprey, FL, 34229.

Launch: Beach launch in Oscar Scherer State Park, which is about ten miles south of Sarasota on U.S. 41. Take the first paved right turn past the entrance station.

Phone: (941) 483-5956

Facilities: See hiking section for more information on Oscar Scherer State Park.

Hours: 8:00 A.M. to sunset

Highlights: Oscar Scherer is a good area to see osprey and eagles and abundant waterbirds and to observe a tidal-creek transition zone between freshwater and saltwater environments.

Blackburn Bay is only about a half mile across and is therefore more protected than bigger bays like Sarasota Bay farther north. The Intracoastal Waterway bisects Blackburn Bay. Most shoreline is developed, although there are still many mangroves trees and remnant tidal marshes.

Fishing can be good on the grass flats along Casey Key and excellent around the small bridge on the east end of Blackburn Causeway.

The channel to South Creek can be tricky to find. You may have to navigate around oyster bars and backtrack, but the channel is navigable

SHORELAND PARK (S-41)

Location: Shoreland Park, west from the U.S. 41 and Shoreland Dr. intersection across from the entrance to Oscar Scherer State Park.

Launch: Shoreland Park, Shoreland Dr., Osprey, west of U.S. 41.

Facilities: No facilities except picnic tables.

Hours: No posted hours, but the park is located in a subdivision with street parking so be considerate when using this park.

Highlights: Shoreland Park is a small pocket park in a developed subdivision, only about a quarter-mile north of South Creek. The only parking is only on neighborhood streets requiring a 100-yard portage to the launch site at the park's west end.

Alternative Launch: Blackburn Point Bridge Park: About a mile north of South Creek at the Blackburn Point Bridge there is a good launch site on the causeway's north side. Parking is available, although there are no restrooms or water. Casey Key Fish House, a restaurant, is across Blackburn Point Road from the park.

NOKOMIS BEACH PARK (S-50)

Location: 901 Casey Key Road, Casey Key, Nokomis 34275.

Facilities: Boat ramp, parking, beach, restrooms, water, concession, restaurants across Albee Road Bridge.

Hours: 6:00 A.M. to midnight.

Launch: Boat ramp and beach launch west side of Casey Key Road just north of Albee Road Bridge.

Highlights: This area is strongly influenced by tidal flow due to its proximity to the Venice Inlet.

About four miles south of Blackburn Causeway, Nokomis Beach marks the southern terminus of Blackburn Bay, a narrow bay about a half-mile wide. Blackburn Bay contains large grass flats, which attract snook. Dolphins may swim next to your boat particularly in the area north of Albee Road Bridge. South Creek flows into Blackburn Bay (See Oscar Scherer State Park). Boat traffic can be very heavy in the Intracoastal Waterway on weekends and holidays. Tidal current can be strong as you approach the Venice Jetties.

DONA BAY/VENICE INLET

NORTH JETTY PARK (S–51)
Location: 1000 Casey Key road, Casey Key, Nokomis.
Phone: (941) 486-2311
Launch site: Beach launch east side of Casey Key Road.
Facilities: Restrooms, water, concession.
Hours: 6:00 A.M. to midnight
Alternative Launch: A nearby launch on the south side of the jetties is at Higel Marine Park at 1204 Tarpon Center Drive, Venice, where there is a boat ramp with limited daytime parking. The only facilities at Higel Marine Park are picnic tables.
Highlights: Venice Inlet connects the Gulf of Mexico with Dona Bay and Roberts Bay. South from Roberts Bay, the Intracoastal Waterway is channelized to Lemon Bay. Jetties stabilize the pass at Venice Inlet. Fishing can be good on tide changes.

CASPERSEN BEACH $\left(\text{S–56}\right)$

Location: 4100 Harbor Drive South, Venice.

Phone: (941) 316-1172

Facilities: Restrooms, water.

Launch: There is no designated launch although on the east side of Harbor Drive along the bay there are several spots suitable for launch.

Hours: 6:00 A.M. to midnight.

Highlights: The sand dunes along the beach give the area a deserted feel. The access road to Caspersen Beach may be partially covered with sand that has blown over small dunes. On the west side of Harbor Drive, a boardwalk winds along the beach; on the east side of Harbor Drive, exotic vegetation that had overgrown the area has now been cleared. The area will appear denuded until the native plants grow back. The shoreline mangroves have made a good recovery. The park only has 113 acres, but in addition to the beach habitat you'll find a salt marsh, a freshwater marsh, mud flats, and a small lake. You will exit the park by boat at the Venice Bypass canal.

MANASOTA BEACH $\left(\text{S–58}\right)$

Location: 8570 Manasota Key Road, Manasota Key.

Phone: (941) 474-8919

Launch: Beach launch on east side of Manasota Key Road or at the boat ramp.

Facilities: Restrooms, water.

Hours: 6:00 A.M. to midnight.

Highlights: This launch site provides excellent access to Lemon Bay. Other than a short boardwalk curling along a tiny bayou by the boat ramp, the primary attraction of this small fourteen-acre park is access to the beach on the Gulf of Mexico and to Lemon Bay.

BLIND PASS BEACH (S–60)

Location: 6725 Manasota Key Road, Manasota Key.

Telephone: (941) 474-8919

Launch: At the east end of the parking lot look for signs directing you south on a dirt road to the shoreline.

Facilities: Restrooms and ample parking.

Hours: 6:00 A.M. to midnight

Highlights: The launch is on a bayou bordering Manasota Key. This section of Lemon Bay south of the park has extensive grass flats where fishing is popular.

LEMON BAY PARK (S–59)

Location: 570 Bay Park Blvd., Englewood. From Old Englewood Road follow signs to the park.

Phone: (941) 474-3065

Launch: On Lemon Bay north of the Environmental Center.

Facilities: Restrooms, water.

Hours: 6:00 A.M. to midnight.

Highlights: Due to well-dispersed access points, a paddler has many choices for routes on Lemon Bay. For example, an excellent day trip could be to paddle from Manasota Beach with a stop at Lemon Bay Park and a final take-out at either Indian Mound Park or Lemon Bay boat ramp.

The two-hundred-acre Lemon Bay Park contains a beautiful longleaf pine forest. This forest appears never to have been timbered. The pine trees are old and gnarly unlike the scrawny second-growth timber common locally. The old trees make the park prime eagle habitat. You are almost guaranteed to see an eagle at this park, especially during nesting season. Several miles of trail meander through the pine forest, which have observation points for eagle nests. In addition, trails follow the shoreline with several observation decks overlooking Lemon Bay.

The pine forest, swamp, marsh, and mangrove habitats are home to a great variety of bird species. The park also has a small butterfly garden. The Sarasota County Parks Department schedules guided nature walks and educational programs there.

INDIAN MOUND PARK (S–61)

Location: 210 Winson Ave., Englewood. From I-75 take Exit 191 toward Englewood. Continue on North River Road, which becomes Dearborn. Near the bay turn south onto West Green Street, then turn right onto Winson Ave.

Phone: (941) 316-1172.

Launch: Boat ramp and beach launch.

Facilities: Restrooms, water available only in restrooms, parking.

Hours: 6:00 A.M. to Midnight

Highlights: This is another park worth a stop while paddling Lemon Bay. A short nature trail goes over the large Indian mound in this one-acre park on the shore of Lemon Bay. Interpretive signs provide some background on the Indians that made the mound. Tropical trees and scrubs grow in and around the mound.

LEMON BAY BOAT RAMP (S–63)

Location: West end of bridge to Englewood Beach on south side of State Road 776.

Launch: Boat ramp.

Facilities: None. Limited parking by the boat ramp, with more available across the bridge toward the mainland on the north side of the causeway.

Hours: No posted hours.

Highlights: Though just south of Sarasota County, this launch provides access for the exploration of Lemon Bay. Stump Pass State Recreation Area is only about two miles south at Stump Pass. The small islands east of Manasota Key can be circumnavigated from this launch. Boat and personal watercraft traffic can be heavy in the area.

STUMP PASS STATE RECREATION AREA (S-64)

Location: South end of Manasota Key at Stump Pass.

Launch: Beach launch east side of parking lot.

Facilities: Restrooms, no drinking fountain, water available only from lavatories, parking. (Parking lot may be full weekends on and holidays). Entrance fee.

Hours: 8:00 A.M. to sunset.

Highlights: Stump Pass is a new state park located at a dynamic pass from the Gulf of Mexico to Lemon Bay. This state recreation area is very popular. While there is parking, expect the lot to be full on weekends and holidays, so arrive early to obtain a spot. Less than three miles south of the Sarasota County line, this park provides excellent access to south Lemon Bay. This pass can be compared to other local passes like Venice Inlet and Midnight Pass. Stump Pass is very dynamic and must be dredged to maintain its navigability.

MYAKKA RIVER

MYAKKA RIVER STATE PARK (S-43)

Location: 13207 State Road 72, Sarasota, FL, 34241. 17 miles east of Sarasota on S.R. 72 (Exit 205 I-75).

Phone: (941) 361-6511

Launch: Boat ramp near the concession stand on the Upper Lake, beach launch at Park Drive Bridge, at the entrance station parking lot (100-yard portage), and at picnic area one mile east of Park Drive Bridge.

Facilities: Both water and restrooms are available at the entrance station and at the concession at the Upper Lake.

Hours: 8:00 A.M. to sunset.

Highlights: See hiking section for a general description of

Myakka River State Park. With several different habitats, Myakka River State Park has some of the best opportunities for wildlife observation in Florida.

At Myakka River State Park you can paddle on the lakes or on the Myakka River, which is easy except during adverse conditions like high wind or water. When the wind is too strong for a lake paddle, the river, protected from the wind, will be calmer. When the water is too high and fast for a river paddle, the Upper Lake can be paddled.

One option in the park is to paddle Upper Myakka Lake and Myakka River from Upper Lake to Park Drive Bridge. The Upper Myakka Lake is very popular due to easy access and canoe rentals at the park concession, phone number (941) 923-1120. A boat ramp and parking lot are just beyond the concession. Birding is excellent around the Upper Lake shoreline, and alligators are ubiquitous. A popular paddle is from the boat ramp west along the lakeshore to the small dam, which marks the outfall of the Myakka River. The dam can be portaged for travel downstream through a grassy wetland and along hammock edges. The paddle from the boat ramp to the Park Drive Bridge is about two to three hours one way depending on water flow. You can either paddle back upstream to the ramp, more difficult than the paddle downstream, or take out at the bridge and shuttle back to the parking lot. If you paddled upstream from the bridge, a lunch or snack break can be taken at the park concession. Boats can be left at the dam for the short walk to the concession. Disadvantages to paddling the Upper Lake are its popularity and noise from the airboats operated by the concessionaire.

The more venturesome and experienced paddler can go to the Lower Lake in the Myakka Wilderness Preserve. You must have a permit to paddle in the Wilderness Preserve, which begins on the Myakka River at the S.R. 72 Bridge and ends at the southern park boundary. Obtain a permit at the entrance station.

You will paddle the Myakka River downstream to the Lower Lake. The return is upstream against the current. The paddle downstream is approximately one hour. Launch either from the Park Drive Bridge or from the entrance station parking lot, which entails a one-hundred-yard portage. Along the river to the Lower Lake you paddle through grass wetlands and hammocks. Note carefully your location when you leave the river and enter the lake. The river entrance can be difficult to find on your return. The Lower Lake is a bonanza for wildlife. Here you will find the largest flocks of ducks and the widest variety of waterbirds in the area. If you are quiet and observant, do not be surprised to see fox, bobcat, or hog. The alligators are thickest in the Lower Lake and the biggest ones congregate there too. Don't be shocked to see eleven- or twelve-footers. A good lunch stop is across the Lower Lake and past big hole on the east bank where the river exits the lake.

Get Involved: The legislature often underfunds the state parks and attempts to privatize more park operations. Inform yourself on these issues and communicate to the governor, your state representative, and senator. The state parks not only preserve a bit of "real Florida," they are major tourist attractions. For example, of tourist attractions that charge fees, Myakka River State Park is the most visited attraction in Sarasota County.

SNOOK HAVEN (S–48)

Location: 5000 Venice Ave. East, Venice. (Turn south from River Road onto a dirt lane).

Phone: (941) 485-7221

Launch: Boat ramp behind Snook Haven restaurant. There is a fee.

Facilities: Restaurant, canoe and kayak rental.

Hours: Opens 7:00 A.M.

Alternative launch: Marina Park, 7030 Chancellor Blvd., North Port, FL 34287. The phone number is (941) 423-2786. Open during daylight hours.

Highlights: Snook Haven is an "old Florida"–style restaurant and bar on the banks of the Myakka River. It is very popular on weekends and holidays. You may have difficulty getting to the launch through the crowds because Snook Haven often hosts bands and other entertainment. At times, especially Sunday afternoons, motorcyclists by the hundreds converge on Snook Haven for food, drink, and good times. Call to learn the event schedule before going to paddle.

From Snook Haven you can either paddle upstream toward the Carlton Reserve and Myakka State Park or downstream to Charlotte Harbor. You will encounter less powerboat traffic upstream. Traveling upstream, you will continue to see development until several miles above the Border Road Bridge. The boundary of the Carlton Reserve is about a mile south of the Border Road Bridge on the east bank. Development on the west bank continues upstream for several more miles. Beyond the development, the river is very scenic as it winds through hammocks. The paddle to Border Road Bridge is about three miles.

Downstream from Snook Haven expect to encounter boat traffic and fishermen. The river continues to be scenic although this stretch is mostly developed with only sporadic undeveloped gaps. Upstream from the U.S. 41 bridge you will reach the tidal transition zone. South of the bridge there is a wood stork rookery. Do not disturb the birds by getting too close.

The Myakkahatchee Creek enters the Myakka River from the east about two miles south from the U.S. 41 bridge. The river bisects the Myakka State Forest, which has a boat dock and landing area about four miles south from the U.S. 41 bridge.

Get Involved: The Littoral Society emphasizes shoreline conservation and sponsors kayaks trips locally.

Join the American Littoral Society:

4154 Keats Dr.

Sarasota FL 34241

(941) 377-5459

MYAKKAHATCHEE CREEK (S–46)

Location: Myakkahatchee Park, 6968 Reisterstown Road, North Port. From I-75 (exit 182) turn north on Sumter Blvd.; turn west on Tropicaire Blvd.; turn north on Reisterstown Road and continue to park entrance on right.

Phone: (941) 486-2706

Facilities: Restrooms and water.

Hours: 8:00 A.M. to 10:00 P.M.

Launch: Shore launch near the entrance.

Highlights: This is the put-in for the Myakkahatchee Creek canoe trail. The trail is scenic, although at times difficult to paddle because the creek is left natural, so trees and brush are not removed. At low water the creek can be marginally navigable. The canoe trail continues south about five miles to Butler Park for take-out at a beach landing. Butler Park is located at 6205 West Price Blvd., North Port. The take-out is beside the ball fields. You will find ample parking, rest rooms, and water.

Butler Park is the last take-out; do not miss it.

Bicycling

Unfortunately, the entire state of Florida is not known as bicycle friendly. Manatee and Sarasota Counties are no exception. Traffic in most areas is heavy. Where traffic is light the roads tend to be narrow. Many automobile drivers are not attentive to bicyclists. Automobile and bicycle crashes are not uncommon in both Sarasota and Manatee Counties. Do not ride without a helmet.

While both counties have some on-road bicycle lanes, do not rely on these bicycle lanes to be safe. In many places, officially marked bicycle lanes are no more than painted lines along the road shoulders that may inexplicably end, or worse, squeeze you into curbs. The bicycle lanes do not connect in any logical manner. Please note, official bicycle lane maps specifically disclaim any representation as to their safety.

Designated bicycle trails may have restrictions that limit their desirability for serious bicycling. For instance, the town of Longboat Key has an ordinance limiting speed to 10 mph on bicycle paths or sidewalks. Longboat Key also requires that you have a bell or horn on your bike.

The awareness that bicycles are not only for recreation, but also for transportation is slowly reaching the public. Both Sarasota County and Manatee County have bicycle coordinators. Funding for bicycle safety and paths is increasing. For instance,

Sarasota County has recently funded bicycle lanes on Siesta Key. Sarasota is working on a rails-to-trail bicycle trail. Encourage these efforts.

Bicycle trail maps can be obtained for Sarasota County from Sarasota County Public Works, Bicycle/Pedestrian Program, (941) 378-6191.

Although not a premier bicycling area with grade A bicycling paths, some scenic and enjoyable on- and off-road bicycling is available. Keep in mind, however, that these rides may be no safer than others you may choose.

MYAKKA RIVER STATE PARK (S–43)
(See hiking section for directions and facilities)

Highlights: A paved road about seven miles long winds through Myakka River State Park, which is excellent for bicycling. There are no designated bike lanes, but traffic is generally slow moving (the speed limit is 25 mph). The park road passes though all the major habitats in the park. Bicycling this road allows you to see the wildlife much better than by car. Because a bike is quiet, bicyclists sometimes get very close to wildlife. Riders have ridden close to pigs, turkeys, snakes, deer, hawks, and owls on the park road. Once a red-shouldered hawk flew up from the roadside beside a biker and continued flying within arm's reach for several yards.

Myakka can also serve as a base for longer rides. Riders can exit the north entrance of the park to ride Clay Gully Road. The countryside along Clay Gully road is sparsely populated and mostly agricultural with light traffic. You can ride east on Clay Gully Road to State Road 70 and retrace to the park entrance for a roundtrip ride of about thirty-five miles, although riding on State Road 70 is not recommended.

An alternative is to ride north as you leave the north park entrance and then turn east on Singletary Road, which will also take you to State Road 70. Usually traffic on this route will be heavier than the Clay Gully route, but it passes over the Myakka River, by the Crowley Nature Center, and through the settlement of Old Myakka. You can extend this ride by crossing State Road 70 and riding the Wauchula Road past Myakka City.

Bicycling from Sarasota to Myakka is not recommended. Clark Road (State Road 72) is very dangerous for bicyclists, and riders have been killed on this route. Also, it is not recommended that you ride Fruitville Road (State Road 780) between I-75 and Verna Road. Fruitville Road is narrow with fast traffic.

Myakka River State Park also has off-road bicycling. Unfortunately, the off-road bicycling can only be characterized as marginal. Many trails are restricted to hiking when they could be multiple-use trails, and many dirt roads are simply impassable in dry weather due to deep sand. The park service also harrows the dirt roads for fire control, making them impractical to ride for several months afterward.

Nevertheless, off-road bicycling can be enjoyable at the park with the right conditions, namely when the park is neither too wet nor too dry. Your best chance for ridable conditions is during winter and spring after a rain. When the unpaved roads are passable, they offer quick access to the park interior. By bike, you can visit areas that cannot be easily hiked in a day.

Get Involved: Support the work of the bicycle coordinators in Sarasota and Manatee Counties. The Sarasota coordinator is Alexander J. Boudreau, P.E., (941) 378- 6191, e-mail aboudrea@co.sarasota.fl.us. The Manatee County coordinator is Troy Salisbury, (941) 748-4501 ext. 6859.

Encourage the development of more and better bicycle trails. For example, a bicycle trail linking Sugar Bowl Road and Singletary Road along State Road 70 would provide a loop ride from Myakka River State Park and return. A bicycle trail to Myakka along State Road 72 could save lives.

Encourage the Park Service at Myakka State Park to use other methods than harrowing, such as mowing, to maintain fire breaks so the dirt roads in the park are not made impassable for bikes.

LONGBOAT KEY/ANNA MARIA

Location: South Longboat Key to Anna Maria and return.

Facilities: A good picnic spot on this route is Joan M. Durante Park at 5500 Gulf of Mexico Drive, Longboat Key. Water and restrooms are available. You can get drinking water from a fountain at Bayfront Park Recreation Center, 4052 Gulf of Mexico Drive, Longboat Key.

Highlights: This ride along the Gulf of Mexico and beaches is exceptionally scenic. While traffic can be heavy, there are bicycle lanes most of the way. Many cyclists like to ride this route early in the morning with a breakfast break in Anna Maria.

Along this route you will have beautiful beach and Gulf views. Several beach access points along Longboat Key are marked. One beautiful stretch of beach along the route is best accessed by bike because there is no parking for cars.

CASEY KEY (S-51)

Location: North Jetty Park, 1000 Casey Key Road, Casey Key, Nokomis, FL, 34275.

Facilities: Restrooms and water at North Jetty Park and also at Nokomis Beach Park along the route.

Highlights: This is a pleasant ride along beachfront and through scenic neighborhoods.

Ride from North Jetty Park to Blackburn Point Park, 800 Blackburn Point Rd, Sarasota or reverse. This short ride (about six miles one-way) is one of the more beautiful rides in the area. For much of the ride, you can enjoy views of the Gulf of Mexico. Almost the entire ride is through beautiful tropically landscaped residential neighborhoods.

The Casey Key Road is narrow, but traffic speeds are low. Be alert for landscaping and service vehicles that park on the roadway. Remember to stay in your lane because there are blind corners. At these corners, approaching bicycles or vehicles can be upon you before you see or hear them.

Get Involved: Encourage Sarasota County to fund a bicycle trail linking Siesta Key and Casey Key across Palmer Point Beach

Park. Let the city and county commissioners know that service vehicles, like lawn maintenance trucks, should not be allowed to block travel lanes and bike paths.

CARLTON RESERVE (S–45)

(See hiking section for a description of the reserve.)

Location: 1800 Mabry Carlton Parkway, Venice, FL.

Telephone: (941) 486-2547

Facilities: Restrooms and water.

Hours: Sunrise to sunset.

Highlights: Carlton Reserve offers off-road bicycling. Over eighty miles of dirt roads meander through the reserve.

Only about three miles of trail are open to the public without a permit. The permit to ride the backcountry may be obtained by calling (941) 486-2547. The dirt road trails can be difficult, if not impossible, to ride during times of high water or drought. Wild hogs are abundant and their rooting sometimes completely destroys long sections of trail. Only the strongest riders can continue through those sections without pushing their bikes. Like Myakka Park, dirt tracks can be harrowed for fire control and become impassable for bikes.

The Myakka River can be accessed by the dirt trails, and some trails parallel portions of the river.

MYAKKAHATCHEE ENVIRONMENTAL PARK (S–46)

(See hiking section for a description of the park.)

Location: 6968 Reisterstown Road, North Port, FL, 34287. From I-75 (exit 182, Sumter Blvd.) take Sumter Road north to Tropicaire Blvd.; turn west and continue to Reisterstown Road. Turn north and continue to park entrance.

Facilities: Restrooms and water.

Hours: 8:00 A.M. to 10:00 P.M.

Highlights: About ten miles of multiple-use dirt trails twist along Myakkahatchee Creek. They connect with Oaks Park and Butler Park downstream. During periods of high water the trails will be impassable. They are often difficult to bike because they are either muddy or sandy in places. Portions of the trail can be almost impassable because they are left mostly natural and untrimmed.

CARTER ROAD PARK

Location: Travel north to Polk County on State Road 37; continue for about 2 1/2 miles from the intersection with State Road 60 in Mulberry to West Carter Road. Turn east on West Carter Road and continue about one mile to the park entrance on the south side of the road.

Phone: Polk County Parks and Recreation, 515 East Blvd. St. Bartow, FL 33830, manages Carter Road Park. Their phone number is (863) 534- 4340.

Facilities: Restrooms and water at the baseball fields. Bicycle trail maps are sometimes available at the kiosk across the street from the baseball fields. The Ridge Riders Mountain Bike Association maintains the trails. Their website, www.ridgeriders.net, has trail maps for the park.

Hours: 7:00 A.M. to 8:00 P.M.

Highlights: While not in Sarasota or Manatee County and about an hour's drive north, this park is included because it is the closest park for "technical" riding with more than six miles of trail. Skilled riding techniques are required to ride the more difficult "single track" trails meandering through an old phosphate pit. Swerving around rocks and trees, some trails can be over twenty feet high along cliffs or steep banks. Even skilled, adventure riders risk tumbles on challenging trails like the one known as "The Beast." Jumping rocks or charging down steep hills, you could be thrown from your bike into a lake. Fortunately, for the less skillful rider, most routes have alternatives. Should you lose your nerve, which is likely somewhere on the tough trails, simply opt for an easier route or walk your bike.

Get Involved:

At this park you can observe the despoliation from phosphate mining. Although the area was mined years ago, the topography and watershed have been greatly altered. Oppose phosphate mining that threatens watersheds.

Join the Sarasota Manatee Bicycle Club, P.O. Box 15053, Sarasota, FL, 34277-1053. Call (941) 358-0297 for membership information.

Walking

Some people define a walk as a short hike. Walking implies that the journey will be easier than a hike, but not always. Perhaps the difference can't be defined, but for purposes of this book it doesn't matter. Just know that for hikes, boots and long pants are recommended. You shouldn't need either for these walks.

Sarasota and Manatee Counties have world-class walks. You cannot find white, crystalline quartz beach sand like that at Siesta Key anywhere else in the world. Few places in the world have sunsets as beautiful as the west coast of Florida. our paradise is blessed with easily accesible habitats where wildlife, sometimes even endangered or threatened species can be observed on a short walk.

EMERSON POINT PARK (N–7)
(See canoeing section for further description.)

Location: 5801 17th St. West, Palmetto. Go west on 10th St. in Palmetto from U.S. 41 and follow signs to Emerson Point Park.

Telephone: (941) 776-2295 or 742-5923

Facilities: Toilets at park entrance.

Hours: Sunrise to sunset.

Highlights: A strategic location straddling Tampa Bay and the Manatee River. Prehistoric Indians lived here and Hernando DeSoto, a Spanish conquistador, landed nearby. This park is worth a visit for the exceptional views of Tampa Bay and the Sunshine Skyway Bridge, but it has much more to offer. The first stop in the park should be the Indian mound near the park entrance. Built by prehistoric Indians, the mound may have served ceremonial purposes. Tropical vegetation like gumbo limbo grows in and around the mound.

Historically Emerson Point was used by Cuban fishermen and was homesteaded by early settlers. The homestead era is still evident in the vegetation planted by early settlers and the ruins of their homes.

A second stop should be the tower on the north side of the entrance drive. From this tower you have an overview of the entire park, Tampa Bay, and the Sunshine Skyway Bridge.

Mangrove forest is the primary habitat in the park. Walking trails wind through the park. Birding is excellent. Expect to see wading birds like great blue herons, little blue herons, and egrets. You may see flocks of wood storks or roseate spoonbills.

BEER CAN ISLAND (N–21)

Location: Northern tip of Longboat Key. Beach access from North Shore Road.

Facilities: None, limited parking.

Hours: 5:00 A.M. to 11:00 P.M.

Highlights: Presently Beer Can Island is not an island, but a spit of land jutting and curling around Longboat Pass from the Gulf of Mexico. Because the spit is a very dynamic beach, storms could again separate the spit from Longboat Key at any time. Seawater often washes over the spit. The wash scours out the brush and small plants leaving clean sand under the mangroves, so walking through the mangrove fringe is relatively easy.

A popular spot for sunning and beachcombing, the beautiful sandy beach and bayou is also an excellent birding location and an Audubon hotspot. Competing for food and space, the seabirds can become quite boisterous in this area.

LONGBOAT KEY BEACHES

N–24 to N–26

Location: Although not always well marked, several beach access points with parking are scattered along Gulf of Mexico Drive at North Shore Road, Broadway, Atlas Street, Longview Drive, Westfield Street, and Mayfield Street.

Facilities: None, limited parking. Beachfront stretches approximately ten miles on Longboat Key, but public access to the beach can be difficult due to the scarcity of public access points with adequate parking. Public access to the beach is particularly poor along the southern portion of Longboat Key. The first access with parking north from New Pass is Mayfield Street. At the Longview Drive access, 3400 Block, Gulf of Mexico Drive, you have public access to both the beach and the bay.

Hours: 5:00 A.M. to 11:00 P.M. (Note that parking hours can be marked as less than the beach hours at some access points. Don't get towed.)

Highlights: Longboat is an uncrowded beach claimed by many to be the most beautiful in the area.

Unlike Siesta Key, walking here is moderately difficult because the sand does not compact well from high tide. When it does compact, the surface tends to slope. Expect your feet to sink into soft sand along most stretches. At times you may have to wade around sea walls that encroach on the beach in a few places.

Due to limited access and more difficult walking conditions, fewer people walk on Longboat than Siesta Key Beach. As a result, you can feel isolated even during tourist season.

Expect to see the birds typically found at the beach, like ibis, plovers and sandpipers. Look for schools of stingrays in the shallows during summer.

SOUTH LONGBOAT KEY QUICK POINT NATURE PRESERVE

N–32

(See canoeing/kayaking section for further description.)

Location: 100 Gulf of Mexico Drive, Longboat Key. Entrance on the west side of Gulf of Mexico Drive at the north end of the New Pass Bridge. Walkway goes under New Pass Bridge to the east side of Gulf of Mexico Drive.

Facilities: None, small parking area.

Hours: 5:00 A.M. to 11:00 P.M.

Highlights: Quick Point Nature Preserve is a 34-acre park on the south tip of Longboat Key, which has a nature trail and boardwalks. Once used as an area to deposit spoil from New Pass dredging, the area has been reclaimed. Tidal lagoons were dug and extensive exotic vegetation eradicated and replaced with native plants and trees. Many years will be required before the native trees return to their natural condition as the exotics are eliminated.

Mangrove forest is the predominant habitat both as mangrove fringe and mangrove swamp. Pleasant paths zigzag along Sarasota Bay shoreline and mangrove forest. Sandy shoreline is interspersed with the fringe mangrove trees. Boardwalks allow access into the red mangrove forest and interior tidal pools. You should see marine organisms like mangrove crabs and horseshoe crabs. Pelicans, cormorants, and warblers are common.

From this park you have excellent views of New Pass, City Island, and mainland Sarasota.

NORTH LIDO BEACH (N–33)

Location: Lido Key, one quarter mile northwest of St. Armands Circle off John Ringling Boulevard.

Facilities: None, limited parking.

Hours: 6:00 A.M. to midnight.

Highlights: This 77-acre public park along New Pass has 3000 lineal feet of Gulf beach and a short nature trail.

South Lido Beach (N–34)

Location: South Lido Park, 2201 Ben Franklin Dr., Sarasota.

Facilities: Restrooms, water, and ample parking.

Hours: 6:00 A.M. to midnight.

Highlights: Explore the beachfront, bayside, and bayou, and pass environments. Although the park only contains 100 acres, it has 640 linear feet of Gulf beach and 3,500 feet of frontage on Big Pass. The park is divided into northern and southern sections. The south section borders Big Pass and the Gulf of Mexico, and the north section borders Brushy Bayou. A nature trail is located in the north section at the east end of Taft Drive.

Siesta Key Beach (N–36)

Location: 948 Beach Road, Siesta Key, FL, 34242.

Facilities: Restrooms, water, concession stand.

Hours: 6:00 A.M. to midnight.

Highlights: Snow-white beach sand stretches for several miles. Siesta Beach is usually the easiest beach to walk in the area because the sand compacts from tidal inundation and the beach slopes less. As a consequence, as the tide drops the packed sand makes for easy walking. Conditions are so good that running on Siesta Beach is quite popular. In fact, the Manasota Track Club uses the beach for sanctioned races and training sessions.

The public beach is not the only portion of the beach accessible to the public on Siesta Key. From the public beach, which is only forty acres with less than one-half mile of lineal beach, you can easily walk north or south for about 1 1/2 miles each way. For a round trip six-mile walk, start at Beach Access # 5 at the intersection of Ocean Blvd. and Beach Road and walk south to Point of Rocks (Beach Access #13) and return. Parking is by permit only at Point of Rocks. For a shorter walk, park at the public beach pavilion; walk in either direction and return.

At some low tides, walks can be extended farther north on Siesta Key past Beach Access #4. At these low tides the packed sand beach extends north to the groins at the end of Avenida Messina (Beach Access #2, parking by permit only). At exceptionally low tides, the packed sand beach may extend to Sarasota Point on Big Sarasota Pass.

Walking Siesta Beach, you may see dolphins, especially near sunrise or sunset. A day without pelicans diving for fish along Siesta Beach is unusual. Other birds commonly seen are terns, gulls, snowy egrets, willets, sanderlings, and plovers.

The only disadvantage to walking Siesta Beach is its popularity. On weekends and holidays the public beach will be jammed. Away from the public beach, the crowds thin rapidly and early mornings and evenings are generally not as crowded.

The public has traditionally walked the entire length of Siesta Beach although the route may cross platted lots in places. You have every right to walk the shoreline across these privately held lots because in Florida the public has access to the shoreline to the mean high water line. Nevertheless, keep in mind that the shoreline below mean high water must be accessed from the water or from public property, not across private property.

TURTLE BEACH/PALMER POINT BEACH (S-37)
(See canoeing/kayaking section for further description)

Location: Turtle Beach is at the south end of Siesta Key on Midnight Pass Road. Palmer Point Beach is at the southern tip of Siesta Key, northern tip of Casey Key.

Phone: (941) 346-3207

Facilities: Restrooms, water, and parking at Turtle Beach. None at Palmer Point Beach.

Hours: 6:00 A.M. to midnight.

Highlights: Turtle Beach is a 14-acre county park with 1,200 linear feet of gulf beach. Palmer Point Beach is a 30-acre county park with 2,400 linear feet of Gulf beach. To reach Palmer Point Beach you must walk the shoreline south from Turtle Beach. This walk can be an adventure because you will probably have to wade to get to Palmer Point Beach. Sarasota County has allowed big rocks to be placed along the shore to protect a condominium from beach erosion. These rocks are your first obstacles. Other obstacles are farther south where the beach has eroded past the foundations of houses. You will also have to wade around them except at the lowest tides. At high tide when the surf is high, this route can be impassable.

When conditions allow, the walk to Palmer Point Beach is worthwhile. Once there you may have the beach to yourself because the only access is by boat or walking. You will be walking the shoreline where Midnight Pass flowed until 1984 when it was closed in an effort to stop the northern migration of the pass, which threatened to wash away homes.

The bay on the east side of Palmer Point can be a productive birding area. Reddish egrets and roseate spoonbills frequent the area. Shelling is as good as any section of beach in Sarasota County.

Get Involved: By walking the shoreline to Palmer Point Beach you can see consequences of building too close to a dynamic shoreline beach. Without construction so near the shore, the big rocks for erosion control would not be necessary. Likewise, had the houses been built farther from the shoreline they would not be washing away. We have not learned from these examples; construction still continues at other locations too close to the shoreline.

Rocks and sea walls along the shoreline make public access to the shoreline difficult if not impossible. Encourage that a public easement be provided anytime shoreline alterations are allowed. Encourage Sarasota County to obtain a public easement connecting Siesta Key and Casey Key for walking and bicycling.

SOUTH JETTY TO STUMP PASS $\boxed{S-51}$
RECREATION AREA

Location: South Jetty Park is at the terminus of Tarpon Center Drive, Venice.

Facilities: At South Jetty Park, there are restrooms, water, concession, and parking.

Hours: 6:00 A.M. to midnight.

Highlights: South Jetty Park provides access to the south jetty at Venice Inlet and access to miles of beach shoreline. From the South Jetty you can walk the beach shoreline south to Stump

Pass, a distance of more than sixteen miles. Yet walking this beach is not easy. The sand does not compact well and the beach is often sloped. The easiest course is often at water's edge as waves recede, so you'll likely get your feet wet. A few seawalls limit walking at high tide, but you can generally wade around them.

Fortunately, walks can be shortened to suit your ambition because this shoreline has numerous access points. The first access point only a half mile south from the jetties is Venice Beach. Venice Beach at 101 The Esplanade, telephone (941) 316-1172, has all beach amenities—restrooms, ample parking, and concession.

About 1 1/2 miles farther south you find Service Club Park at 1600 Harbor Drive South, telephone (941) 316-1172. Dune walkovers and boardwalks provide access from the beach to restrooms and water. This seven-acre park has scrub habitat that comes right to the beach dunes. Surprisingly, scrub jays still survive in this urban park next to the Venice Airport. Among the palmetto thickets you may see a gopher tortoise. If you walk around the unmarked trails, watch for snakes and lizards. Do not feed the scrub jays.

The next access a half mile farther south is Brohard Beach at 1600 Harbor Drive South, Venice, telephone (941) 316-1172. To continue walking south you'll have to duck under the Venice Municipal Pier. A popular fishing locale, the pier has restrooms, snack bar, bait shop, and Sharky's On The Pier restaurant.

Less than a mile farther south you reach Caspersen Beach, 4100 Harbor Drive South, Venice. Harbor Drive dead-ends in the park. You can not drive south of the parking lot because the lower portion of this 113-acre park has been left in its natural state. At Caspersen Beach, you will probably see people sifting sand for fossilized sharks' teeth and shells. Caspersen Beach is designated as a National Seashore.

Continuing south four miles you'll find Manasota Beach at the west end of Manasota Beach Road, 8570 Manasota Key Road, Manasota Key. Telephone (941) 474-8919. This park has restrooms and parking.

Another 2 1/2 miles south and you reach Blind Pass Beach, 6725 Manasota Key Road, Manasota Key. Telephone (941) 474-

8919. Restrooms and ample parking are available. On the park's bay side mangroves line the shore and curve around a scenic bayou.

Your next access to the shoreline is Englewood Beach about 3 1/2 miles from Blind Pass Beach where restrooms are available.

Two miles farther south the beach shoreline ends at Stump Pass Recreation Area at the south end of Manasota Key Road. Restrooms are available, parking is limited.

There are few places in the country with reasonable public access where you can walk more than sixteen miles of shoreline. Along this beach walk you not only have the opportunity to see shore birds like gulls, terns, sandpipers, and plovers, but you also have the opportunity to see ducks and wading birds in the parks. As a bonus you might see uncommon upland birds like scrub jays or eagles.

MYAKKA RIVER STATE PARK (S-43)
(See the hiking section for description.)
Location: 13207 S.R. 72, Sarasota, FL 34241
Phone: (941) 361-6511
Facilities: Restrooms at entrance station, concession stand at Upper Myakka Lake, and Clay Gully picnic area.
Highlights: Myakka River State Park can be enjoyed on foot without hiking the backcountry. Surprisingly, you may see more wildlife walking popular areas of the park because the wildlife are accustomed to people there. For instance, river otters have been seen on the nature trail, and turkey are sometimes spotted on the park road.

You have several choices for good walks that provide an excellent overview of most habitats found in the park. The shoulders of the paved road through the park are well suited for walking. Traffic moves slowly and is generally light except on weekends and holidays. North Drive past the Big Flat Campground usually has the least traffic. This section is particularly pleasant because you are generally shaded by the trees, but you still have good views of Upper Myakka Lake and marsh habitat. A good destination is the bird walk about 3 1/2 miles from the intersection of Park Drive and North Drive. Along this walk you will see a myriad of wading birds. In addition, you may see osprey and sandhill cranes. Coots and ducks are common especially in winter. From the bird walk, the swallow-tailed kite, one of the world's most beautiful birds, can sometimes be seen.

Certainly take the short walk to the canopy walkway and tower. Located at the nature trail off Park Drive, the tower rises seventy feet. From that height you get excellent views of the forest canopy, riverine marsh, and meandering Myakka River. The nature trail winds through oak hammock, palmetto thickets, and across a slough and depression marsh. Early in the morning you may see deer and hogs along the trail.

SHAMROCK PARK AND NATURE CENTER (S–57)
Location: 4100 West Shamrock Drive, Venice, FL.
Phone: (941) 486-2706
Facilities: Restrooms, ample parking with handicapped-accessible trail.
Hours: Sunrise to sunset.
Highlights: Shamrock Park is a designated natural area park with a 1.2-mile paved nature trail, which circles through coastal scrub and scrubby flatwoods habitats. A large area has been filled with spoil from the dredging of the Intracoastal Waterway. Several scrub jay families live in the park and gopher tortoises have colonized the spoil areas. The park borders the Intracoastal Waterway Venice bypass canal. Rock revetment along the shoreline prohibits boat access.

LEMON BAY PARK (S–59)
Location: 570 Bay Park Blvd., Englewood, FL.
Phone: (941) 474-3065
Hours: 6:00 A.M. to midnight.
Highlights: Lemon Bay Park is a designated natural area park excellent for walking. Wide shell walkways circle through

several habitat types and along the bay front in this 195-acre park. The remnant pine forest and palmetto thickets typify how the countryside here may have looked before development for agriculture and housing. Other habitats in the park are marsh, mangrove, and bay shoreline. The tall pine trees provide nesting sites for bald eagles.

MYAKKAHATCHEE PARK (S–46)

Location: 6968 Reisterstown Road, North Port, FL

Phone: (941) 486-2706

Hours: 8:00 A.M. to 10:00 P.M.

Highlights: A designated natural area park, this 160-acre park is bisected by the Myakkahatchee Creek. Multiple-use dirt trails follow both creek banks. On the north side of the creek the trail is shaded by oak hammock. On the south side, the trail is more open. In addition to hammock, marsh and the creek habitats provide variety attractive to different bird species. Expect to see woodpeckers, warblers, cardinals, blue jays, and bluebirds. Trails can be flooded or overgrown in places.

VENETIAN WATERWAY PARK (S–61)

Location: A proposed ten-mile linear trail along both sides of the Intracoastal Waterway.

Phone: (941) 488-2236

Facilities: This trail is under development with only two short sections complete.

Highlights: When complete this trail will connect downtown Venice to Caspersen Beach. This will be outstanding for walking or biking. Call to verify the progress of the trail.

Get Involved: You can volunteer to help build the trail at (941) 496-8466.

American Littoral Society
4154 Keats Dr.
Sarasota, FL 34241
(941) 377-5459
www.americanlittoralsoc.org

Coast Guard Rescue
(941) 794-3011

Division of Forestry
Florida Department of
  Agriculture and
  Consumer Services
3125 Conner Blvd.
Tallahassee, FL 32399
(850)488-8180
(850)921-8305
www.fl-dof.com

Florida Department of
  Environmental Protection
  Florida Greenways and
  Trail System

3900 Commonwealth Blvd.
Mail Station 795
Tallahassee, FL 32399-3000
(850) 488-3701
www.floridadep.org/gwt

Florida Department of
  Environmental Protection
Florida Park Service
3900 Commonwealth Blvd.
Tallahassee, FL 32399-3000
(850) 488-9872
www.dep.state.fl.us/parks

Florida Sea Kayaking
  Association
www.fska.org/
Florida Trail Association
P.O. Box 13708
Gainesville FL 34949
(904) 229-4700
www.fta.org

Friends of Oscar Scherer
  Park Inc.
1843 S. Tamiami Trail
Osprey, FL 34229

Friends of the Myakka
  River, Inc.
1312 S. Orange Ave.
Sarasota, FL 34239
www.myakka.sarasota.fl.us/
  friends.html
myakka@netsrq.com

Hillsborough County
  Parks and Recreation
1102 East River Cove Drive
Tampa, FL 33604
(863) 975-2160

Kayak Explorers
(Kayaking club)
(941) 924-8654

Manatee County
  Chamber of Commerce
222 10th St. W.
Bradenton, FL 34205
(941) 748-3411

Manatee County Parks
  and Recreation
5502 33rd Ave. Dr. West
Bradenton, FL 34209
(941) 742-5923

Manatee-Sarasota Sierra Club
P.O. Box 3485
Sarasota, FL 34230-3485
www.sierraclub.org/chapters/fl
/sarasota

Mote Marine Laboratory
1600 Ken Thompson Parkway
Sarasota, FL 34236
(813) 388-4441
www.marinelab.sarasota.fl.us

Myakka River State Park
132 S.R. 72
Sarasota, FL 34241
(941) 361-6511
www.myakka.sarasota.fl.us.
myakka@netsrq.com

Pelican Man's Bird Sanctuary
1708 Ken Thompson Parkway
Sarasota, FL 34236
(941) 388-4444
www.pelicanman.org

Ridge Riders Mountain Bike
  Association
6735 Lemon Tree Drive
Lakeland, FL 33813
rrmba@tampabay.rr.com

Sarasota Audubon
  Society, Inc.
P.O. Box 15423
Sarasota, FL 34277-1423
www.audubon.org/chapter/fl/
  sarasota/

Sarasota Bay National
  Estuary Program
5333 North Tamiami Trail
Suite 104
Sarasota, FL 34234
(941) 359-5841
www.sbnep@gte.net

Sarasota County Parks
and Recreation
Main Office: Twin Lakes Park
6700 Clark Road
Sarasota, FL 34241
(941) 316-1172
www.co.sarasota.fl.us

Sarasota Manatee Bicycle Club
P.O. Box 15053
Sarasota, FL 34277-1053

Sarasota Visitor's Center
655 Tamiami Trail North
Sarasota, FL 34236
(941) 957-1877

Southwest Florida Water
Management District
2379 Broad Street
Brooksville, FL 34609-6899
(904) 796-7211
(800) 423-1476
www.swfwmd.state.fl.us

Tampa Bay Sea Kayakers
www.clubkayak.com/tbsk/

Tampa BayWatch, Inc.
8401 Ninth St. North
Suite 230-B
St. Petersburg, FL33702
Telephone: (727) 896-5320
www.tampabaywatch.org

Venetian Waterway Park
257 Tamiami Trail North,
Venice, FL 34285
(941) 488-2236
www.vabi.org

MAPS

The Sarasota Manatee Bicycle Club has ride maps posted on the
Internet at www.bicycleclub.org

The Southwest Florida Water Management District posts its
Recreation Guide with maps at www.swfwmd.state.fl.us/recguide

Manatee County publishes an excellent booklet with good maps,
A Guide to Area Canoe and Kayak Trails. (941) 741-5923

Around the Bend
  Nature Tours
1815 Palma Sola Blvd.
Bradenton, FL34209
www.aroundbend.com
karen@aroundbend.com
(941) 798-8773

Bradenton Bicycle and Kayak
5342 Gulf Dr.
Holmes Beach, FL 34217
(941) 778-7757 and
(941) 779-2453
www.bikayak.com
info@bikayak.com

Economy Tackle Watersports
  Center and Dolphin Dive
  Center
6018 Tamiami Trail S.
Sarasota, FL 34231
(941) 922-9671
www.floridakayak.com/
hurxthal@netsrq.com

Florida Watersports
12507 Cortez Road West
Bradenton, FL 34215
(941) 798-3721
www.cortezfishingcenter.com
floridawatersports@
webtv.com

Island Style Kayak Excursions
2801 North Tamiami Trail
Sarasota, Florida 34234
(941) 365-3892

Kayak Treks
3667 Bahia Vista St.
Sarasota, FL 34232
(941) 365-3892
www.kayaktreks.com
info@kayaktreks.com

Myakka River Outpost
State Road 72
Sarasota, FL 34241
(941) 923-1120

Ray's Canoe Hideaway on the
  Manatee River Kayak Center
1247 Hagle Park Road, NE.
Bradenton, FL 34202
(941) 747-3909
www.rayscanoehideaway.com

Silent Sports of Florida
2301 Tamiami Trail N.
Sarasota, FL 34234
(941) 966 5477

Walk on the Wild Side
3434 N. Tamiami Trail
Suite 817
Sarasota, FL 34234
(941) 351-6500
www.walkwild.com
walkonthewild@aol.com

BOATING CHECKLIST

1. Personal flotation devices (PFDs)
2. Visual distress signals (day and night)
3. Sound-producing device
4. Navigation lights
5. VHF radio
6. Navigation charts
7. Compass
8. Bailer
9. Sponge
10. Extra paddle
11. Bow and stern lines
12. Anchor with sufficient line for anticipated water depth (seven times water depth)
13. Flashlight
14. First aid kit
15. Pump
16. Sponge
17. Survival knife
18. Paddle float
19. Water
20. Signal mirror
21. Sunscreen
22. Clothing adequate for anticipated conditions (As a minimum, always have sufficient clothing for sun protection)
23. Hat and sunglasses
24. Shoes or booties
25. Spray skirt
26. Weather forecast
27. Float plan (Let someone know your departure point, destination, and anticipated return time.)
28. Cellular phone (not a substitute for a marine VHF radio; rather a supplemental safety device and convenience)
29. GPS unit (not a supplement for a chart and compass)

The Sierra Club

The Sierra Club is a "get up and go, get out and do" environmental organization. The Manatee/Sarasota group has an active outings group, which sponsors local outings and also ventures across the country and abroad. The Sierra Club outings group recognized that although there are many outdoor recreation opportunities available in Sarasota and Manatee Counties, some are of these are not well known, and information about specific sites and resources was not readily available from a single source. This booklet fills the gap, exploring the facilities and possibilities in the two counties.

If you are interested in learning about the club's local outings, many to places listed in these pages, pick up an issue of the *Boca-Sierra*, the club newsletter. Listings can also be found on the club's website at www.sierraclub.org/chapters/fl/sarasota. People familiar with both local ecology and the activity generally lead outings. You are welcome to join outings without being a Sierra Club member.

Applications for membership in the club can be obtained at Manatee-Sarasota Chapter, Sierra Club, P.O. Box 3485 Sarasota, and Fl 34230-3487 or at www.sierraclub.org/chapters/fl/sarasota.

By supporting the Sierra Club you help protect the environment and quality of life in Sarasota and Manatee Counties. Of course, there are other ways to contribute to these goals and some are suggested in the "Get Involved" section.

Index of Sites

If you enjoyed reading this book, check out these other Pineapple Press titles. To request our complete catalog or to place an order, write to Pineapple Press, P.O. Box 3889, Sarasota, Florida 34230, or call 1-800-PINEAPL (746-3275). Or visit our website at www.pineapplepress.com.

Alligator Tales by Kevin M. McCarthy. True and tongue-in-cheek accounts of Florida alligators. Filled with amusing black-and-white photos and punctuated by a full-color section. ISBN 1-56164-158-8 (pb)

Bicycling in Florida by Tom Oswald. Divided by region, this book outlines 71 rides including complete directions, maps, and pertinent information. ISBN 1-56164-161-8 (pb)

The Climate and Weather of Florida by James A. Henry, Kenneth M. Portier, and Jan Coyne. In-depth, clear explanations of Florida's weather. ISBN 1-56164-036-0 (hb); 1-56164-037-9 (pb)

The Exploring Wild Florida series: A set of field guides, each with information on all the parks, preserves, and natural areas in its region:

> *Exploring Wild North Florida* by Gil Nelson. From the Suwannee River to the Atlantic shore, and south to include the Ocala National Forest. ISBN 1-56164-091-3 (pb)
> *Exploring Wild Northwest Florida* by Gil Nelson. The Florida Panhandle, from the Perdido River in the west to the Suwannee River in the east. ISBN 1-56164-086-7 (pb)
> *Exploring Wild South Florida,* Third Edition by Susan D. Jewell. From Hobe Sound and Punta Gorda south to include the Keys and the Dry Tortugas. Expanded edition covers Broward, Hendry, Lee, and Palm Beach Counties as well as Dade, Collier, and Monroe. ISBN 1-56164-262-2 (pb)

Guide to the Lake Okeechobee Area by Bill and Carol Gregware. The first comprehensive guidebook to this area of the state. ISBN 1-56164-129-4 (pb)

Myakka by P.J. Benshoff. What's there to do in Myakka River State Park, the largest state park in Florida? This book takes you on dozens of adventures into this wild area, from shady oak hammocks up into aerial gardens, down the wild and scenic river, and across a variegated canvas of prairies, piney woods, and wetlands. ISBN 1-56164-254-1 (pb)

Sea Kayaking in Florida by David Gluckman. This guide to sea kayaking in Florida for novices and experienced paddlers alike includes information on wildlife, camping, and gear; maps of the Big Bend Sea Grasses Saltwater Paddling Trail; tips on kayaking the Everglades; lists of liveries and outfitters; and more. ISBN 1-56164-071-9 (pb)